Instructor's Manual to Accompany

Down to Earth Sociology

Instructor's Manual to Accompany

Down to Earth Sociology

Introductory Readings
SIXTH EDITION

JAMES M. HENSLIN, Editor

Prepared by
Linda K. Henslin and James M. Henslin

THE FREE PRESS
A Division of Macmillan, Inc.
NEW YORK

Collier Macmillan Canada
TORONTO

Maxwell Macmillan International
NEW YORK   OXFORD   SINGAPORE   SYDNEY

The Free Press
A Division of Macmillan, Inc.
866 Third Avenue, New York, N.Y. 10022

Collier Macmillan Canada, Inc.
1200 Eglinton Avenue East
Suite 200
Don Mills, Ontario M3C 3N1

Printed in the United States of America

printing number

1 2 3 4 5 6 7 8 9 10

CONTENTS

NOTE: In this new manual, the <u>Suggestions for Classroom Activities</u> and <u>Test Questions</u> are <u>separate</u> sections.

The "down to earth" quality of an article was foremost in my mind as I made the selection for this Sixth Edition. By this I mean that I chose articles that use a minimum of sociological jargon and quantification to communicate sociological principles, keeping us from losing sight of the people being written about. These articles are not only inherently interesting to students, but they also provide excellent sociological analyses of what lies behind the common features of our social world. They stimulate students to examine the structural bases of social interaction and social relationships.

Beginning students enter the introductory sociology class with a vast background of valuable firsthand "sociological" information. Before ever taking a course in sociology, they have already had much experience with what sociology is all about. For example, they have been exposed to cultural aspects of trust, communication, deviance, sex roles, occupations, death and dying, social change, and social mobility. Furthermore, they have directly and indirectly experienced both the institutions and the social problems of our society. By presenting analyses of areas of life with which students already have some familiarity, these selections build upon their experiences and introduce them to a sociological approach to understanding social life.

Purposely chosen to reflect aspects of American society, Down to Earth Sociology is also suited for general courses in American society or as the sociological component for interdisciplinary courses.

We open the book, then, with selections that promise that sociology will provide a markedly different perspective of a world long familiar and taken for granted. To provide a better foundation for understanding, we also compare and contrast sociology with the other social sciences. In Part II, we continue to lay this foundation by looking at how sociologists do research. We then move in Part III to selections that analyze this familiar world, such as care of the body, the American way of celebrating Christmas, and presenting the self in everyday life. In part IV we examine early socialization and sex roles, continuing to uncover many of the taken-for-granted, and therefore invisible, factors that underlie our everyday social interaction. From these eye-opening analyses of fundamental aspects of everyday life, in Part V we examine interaction in various contexts--on the street, in the doctor's office, at work on city streets and in factories, and in shelters for the homeless--seeing how the basic social structure in which we are immersed affects our perceptions and our behavior.

In Part VI we turn to the topic of conformity by presenting an analysis of social deviance and social control. We especially focus on the process of becoming deviant, of adjusting to one's own deviant activities, and of being set on a course of social events that either moves people farther into deviance or pushes them toward conformity. In Part VII we then turn the sociological lens to stratification, focusing first on those who possess great wealth, followed immediately by a contrastive look at the circumstances of poverty; then on sexual and racial discrimination. Examining the social structure that underlies social inequality, we see that it pits person against person, male against female, and as an unforgettable lesson, we close

4

this section by looking at the socially approved hatred, cruelty, and death that social inequality can engender. Following this, Part VIII presents selections that analyze our social institutions. We look at education, the family, religion, sports, medicine, the law, and the merged interests of the political, economic, and military sectors of our society. In the concluding section we focus on social change, looking especially at changing technology and decision-making in the world of work.

Reflecting a major tension in sociology, the Sixth Edition emphasizes both individual situations and social structure. To focus solely on the structure is to miss people, while to focus only on individual experiences is to miss the social structure that shapes people's experiences.

These articles lend themselves well as guides to help students become involved in doing their own original "field" research. Instead of assigning the traditional library research paper, you might ask students to investigate further some of the topics covered by the articles. For example, students can observe how people from different social backgrounds or group memberships present the self--such as by their clothing and linguistic differences. They can examine how they vary among occupational or ethnic groups, males and females, children and adults, people from different social classes, and so on. Or they can describe the social interaction in different jobs at which they have worked or in the friendship or peer groups of which they have been a part. They can recount their own experiences with deviance, or with racism or sexism, and applying ideas from the appropriate articles examine features of those experiences. Or they can analyze their interaction in the family, the military, the doctor's office, or on city streets. Other articles can be applied to the changes students have undergone in recent years as they have been exposed to new experiences--focusing perhaps on the turmoil of the teen years through which most have just come (or are only now completing), or the complexities of personal adjustment that the college experience itself poses.

If this possibility is mentioned to students when they first begin to use Down to Earth Sociology, they can read the articles with this in mind, and with guidance, their understanding of sociology will be greatly enhanced as they apply these authors' analyses to their own experiences and life situation. This approach also helps make sociology more "down to earth," for it removes sociological principles from the abstract. When given such an opportunity, I have found that students, after asking initial questions and seeking instruction, are highly creative in applying these studies. Such an approach makes the articles come alive to students as they better see their relevance to their own lives and gain new understanding of their own experiences.

The "Suggestions for Classroom Activities" should also contribute to the down-to-earth character of your course and help make the teaching experience more pleasant and rewarding. For each article I have also included multiple-choice, true-false, and essay questions. Using the even-numbered true-false and multiple-choice questions one time and the odd-numbered the next, you can give two different objective tests on each article. Or, by giving few questions, you can develop four or more different tests on each article, each covering material throughout the article. Note that questions are also provided for the introductions to the articles, as well as for the introductions to the major Parts of the book.

5

Finally, since some instructors may wish to reorganize materials around their own preferred conceptual scheme, I have provided a topical index for the selections.

James M. Henslin
Department of Sociology
Southern Illinois University
Edwardsville, Illinois 62026

INDEX TO SUGGESTIONS FOR CLASSROOM ACTIVITIES AND TEST QUESTIONS

The "Suggestions for Classroom Activities" contain many exercises that utilize a small group format. Based on my experience in the classroom, this approach works very well with students at the introductory level. While I cannot provide any magical formula for this teaching format, I can share my own experiences, which are quite modifiable according to your own background and desires.

I first wish to stress that the format I describe below is much more effective when the students have read the assignment. This provides them a "shared stock of knowledge" on which they can build during their discussions. In order to help assure that students do their readings as they come due, instead of waiting until the night before a test to cram 20 articles into their heads, I give regular quizzes. These are not "pop" quizzes, for I give a quiz each class period over the day's reading assignment. Each quiz consists of 5 multiple-choice questions taken from the instructor's manual. The students know what to expect, and they come to class prepared.

Giving the Assignment

I first provide the entire class with a specific assignment, such as, "Compare your experiences with racism (sexism, socialization, observations of X or Y, etc.) with those presented by (name of author) or in (X article)." Without having a specific task on which to focus, small groups often are a waste of time. Numerous examples of such specific tasks are provided in the following pages.

I find that giving the instructions before students break into groups is preferable because when they first enter the groups some students begin "premature interaction" (i.e., they chat and fail to pay attention). In addition, at this latter time I find myself competing with lingering shuffling noises as the students are getting adjusted to their groups.

How to Divide Students into Groups

Should the groups be self-selecting or should students be assigned to groups? I have found that this generally makes little difference, and that students prefer to have a choice in the matter. I also have found that group size is extremely important: Groups smaller than 5 do not have enough variety of ideas to carry on the task, while groups larger than 8 tend to become distracted. Accordingly, I simply announce to the class that they are going to break up into groups, that they may sit with whom they wish, and that no group is to be smaller than 5 or larger than 8. (On rare occasions, I have found it necessary to make group assignments in order to separate certain students, such as "best friends," who find topics other than the assignment more interesting.)

For some topics, however, it is desirable to assign students to groups. I find this to be the case when it comes to exploring topics specifically relating to gender and marital status. In such cases, students appear to find greater freedom in talking to others who share similar background and perception. For my part, this arrangement makes it easier to directly contrast the students' experiences during the "wrap-up." (See the section on "wrap-up" below.)

11

In short, where applicable, such assigning to groups contributes to everyone's learning. For example, due to their unique experiences males and females often hold contrasting points of view. By dividing the class into male and female discussion groups (without assigning anyone to a speciic group), students tend to formulate a more coherent point of view. This then offers the instructor the opportunity to point out these contrasts during the "wrap-up," and then to directly relate them to the relevant backgrounds. A benefit of this technique is that it facilitates growth of the students' sociological imagination.

How Much Time?

I usually allot about 15 minutes for meeting in small groups. I have found that students have difficulty in handling their assignment in less time than this, while they tend to get off the track after about 15 minutes. Fifteen minutes is only a general guideline, however, and is never precisely held to, as students become so wrapped up in some topics that it is not good teaching to break them away. On occasion, students find a topic less engaging, and 10 minutes is sufficient. In some instances I utilize a series of interrelated topics, one immediately following the other, and for this tactic a shorter period keeps the momentum going. The "Suggestions for Classroom Activities" contain suggestions for such series of interrelated topics.

The Empty Chair Technique

I have developed an "empty chair" technique that works quite well. I instruct each group to pull into their circle an extra student desk, which they are to leave empty. This provides me a place to sit as I circulate among the groups. It enables me to enter any group I desire with a minimum of disruption to the group's discussion. It also informs the group members that I may be present in their midst at any time. From a symbolic interaction perspective, this technique provides the symbolic presence of the instructor even during his or her physical presence in another group.

Circulating and Listening

From my experience, it is essential that the instructor circulate among the groups. This communicates the instructor's interest in the topic and involvement in the class. It also helps keep students on the topic. No group ever knows which group I will visit next. In addition, listening to the students discuss the topic informs me about their concerns and orientations, which provide invaluable "jumping off" points for my teaching.

For circulating among the groups, I have made a rule for myself: to listen, to nod, and to move students back onto the topic (which seldom is necessary), but to _never_ contribute to the discussion. These are the _students'_ groups, requiring their effort and involvement. I often find it difficult to not contribute to the groups, for the temptation to "share my wisdom" is strong (the tongue does want to keep moving!). If the instructor talks, however, the students will come to expect the instructor to take over a group when he or she appears. The groups will then take on a different character.

Consequently, I find it best to refrain from talking at this point, much better to listen and learn, to save everything for the "wrap-up."

Acceptance and Participation

I have also found it essential to foster an atmosphere of acceptance. While I encourage questions and discussion even during lectures, and facilitate these by letting students know they will not be "put down," even obliquely, these small groups are the students' groups, where the purpose is for students to share with one another. If the instructor structures a total atmosphere of acceptance (students can express any opinion, no matter how outrageous the instructor may find it), even shy students participate well.

An added benefit of this approach is that it allows the instructor to become familiar with at least a segment of the diversity of opinions held by the class. On occasion, you will note that students find themselves free to express opinions that, though strongly held, ordinarily are not shared in the classroom setting. Similarly, some students find themselves comfortable enough to share highly personal experiences, such as sexual exploitation in the family. Such sharing of opinions or experiences not only makes for stimulating classes, but, occurring within a focused context, also allows the instructor to uniquely demonstrate the relevance of the sociological materials under discussion.

The Wrap-Up

After the class has met the allotted time (with flexibility), I have them reformulate as a class of the whole. I do this simply by announcing to the entire class that they must conclude their discussion in two more minutes. I then tell them when they have only another minute remaining, and then when the time is up.

During these last couple of minutes, I usually go to the teacher's desk and begin preparations for the wrap-up. This may consist only of writing headings on the blackboard, or it may include jotting down notes on what I have heard or observed in the discussion groups, items that I wish to make certain are fed (with my comments) back to the class.

I usually hear rather interesting comments from students during their discussions, and during the wrap-up I wish to congratulate some students on their insight (e.g., "You are going to make good sociologists!"), while I want to make certain that other comments are corrected. I never indicate a particular student when it comes to correction (acceptance!) and, if necessary, I disguise the comment in order to get at its underlying principle. For insightful comments, I may or may not attribute authorship, depending on my evaluation of what it will accomplish—as well as my memory of who said what!

The wrap-up is essential to the pedagogical success of the small group format. I wish to stress that it is not sufficient to let the class conclude while students are still in the small groups. During the wrap-up, the instructor again becomes the focus of the class as he or she brings everything together. This is the time to sum up student discussions, conclusions, and observations. In addition, through comments, analyses, and interpretations, it is also the opportunity to tie things together by directly relating them to the reading assignment and other literature. In other words, the wrap-up provides the opportunity not only for a summation of the students' experiences but also for the presentation of a mini-lecture in which you have stimulated high student interest.

The way I handle the wrap-up is like this. After the class as a whole has reformulated (with students remaining seated in their groups but now turned toward the front of the classroom), I point to one of the groups and ask them for their most significant conclusion or observation. ("What was the main thing you found?") I usually summarize what they say on the blackboard, perhaps developing headings as I continue. Usually only with an encouraging comment on what was said ("That's interesting" or "That's good"), but refraining from making an analytical response at this moment, I then indicate another group and ask for their most significant point. I continue like this until all groups have contributed and until ideas are exhausted. With this strategy, an informal and unspoken standard of performance comes into being as students learn that they are accountable to the instructor and class for what transpires during the discussion segment. This helps the students to be motivated to participate actively in the small groups.

At this point many ideas have been listed on the blackboard. Sometimes I already have added headings, at other times I do so now. These headings serve as organizational devices to help students better grasp the coherency of these materials. I then "comment" on what the students have come up with. "Comment" is a rather informal descriptor, for what is happening is a "mini-lecture." It is now that I provide the "coherency," the tie-ups between the disparate points made by the students, and the tie-ins of these experiential materials with the sociological literature. (Although one loses the "safety" that comes with the already-prepared, written lecture notes, and there always persists an uncertainty about the particulars that the wrap-up will take, experience will cause the wrap-up to lose its threat and to become an effective and rewarding teaching form.)

Students are highly motivated to follow such a presentation, for those are their experiences and observations that you are discussing. You may also find it useful at the beginning of the term to instruct students to take notes during the wrap-up because what you cover is likely to appear in some way on an upcoming test. (The carrot and the stick?) Otherwise, some students, not used to the spontaneity and informality of such lecturing, and failing to recognize it for what it is, will not put the information down in an organized fashion for later study.

Other Settings

Although this small group format lends itself well to teaching from the readings in this book, it can be utilized in a number of other situations. Small groups are sometimes especially useful to use immediately preceding a lecture in order to stimulate an exchange of ideas which the instructor can contrast during the lecture itself. ("Although I heard you say X or Y, empirical research, however, indicates that...")

This format also is sometimes useful in order to get immediate feedback on some point in a standard lecture. After you have made a presentation on some specific point, for example, students can explore that idea in small groups. You can then see the extent of their understanding (or misunderstanding), and build on it (or modify it).

This approach is especially effective following the presentation of lecture materials on some controversial topic.

Conclusion

In summary, I have found the small group format to be highly successful, and I continue to use it in my classes. I only stumbled upon this strategy through the desire to improve my teaching and to utilize techniques that effectively involve students in the instructional process. I have found that this teaching/learning format is an excellent supplement to the lecture's passive, primarily one-way dissemination of information. In addition to covering the assigned readings, by tapping the students' varied backgrounds and experiences it makes for a livelier class, heightens student interest, breaks down barriers between students, and because students appreciate this more involving format, the classroom experience itself is more enjoyable and successful.

It is my hope that this presentation of what I have developed over the years through trial and error will help you to be more successful in the classroom.

TOPICAL INDEX

If you wish to present the articles in a different order from that of the book, the following classification by major emphases may be of help.

41. The Abolition of El Cortito / Murray

Gender
   6. Doing Fieldwork Among the Yanomamo / Chagnon
  11. On Becoming Male / Henslin
  12. Sexuality and Gender in Children's Daily Worlds / Thorne and
          Luria
  13. Womanspeak and Manspeak / Henley, Hamilton, and Thorne
  14. Self-Fulfilling Stereotypes / Snyder
  34. Confessions of a Househusband / Roache
  35. The Myth of Male Helplessness / Roache
  39. Police Accounts of Normal Force / Hunt

Institutions
   Economic (Also See Work)
  27. The Bohemian Grove and Other Retreats / Domhoff
  31. Tally's Corner / Liebow
  43. New Worlds of Computer-Mediated Work / Zuboff

   Education
  30. The School at Society Corner / Fields and Fields
  33. Learning the Student Role / Gracey
  38. The Cloak of Competence / Haas and Shaffir

   Family
  34. Confessions of a Househusband / Roache
  35. The Myth of Male Helplessness / Roache
  44. Searching for Roots in a Changing World / Rodriguez

   Law
  23. The Saints and the Roughnecks / Chambliss
  25. The Pathology of Imprisonment / Zimbardo
  39. Police Accounts of Normal Force / Hunt

   Medicine
  18. The Vaginal Examination/ Henslin and Biggs
  26. On Being Sane in Insane Places / Rosenhan
  38. The Cloak of Competence / Haas and Shaffir

   Military
  40. The Structure of Power in American Society / Mills

   Political
  27. The Bohemian Grove and Other Retreats / Domhoff
  32. Good People and Dirty Work / Hughes
  40. The Structure of Power in American Society / Mills

   Religion
  36. The Streetcorner Preacher / Hong and Dearman

Methods Used
   Archives (Published Data)
  10. Extreme Isolation / Davis
  17. Sympathy in Everyday Life / Clark
  22. The Survivors of F-227 / Henslin

17

Sex Roles (See Gender)

Social Class

Social Interaction

Social Mobility

Social Problems

Social Structure (Also See Social Class)

SUGGESTIONS FOR CLASSROOM ACTIVITIES

Article 1. Berger, "Invitation to Sociology"

1. In small groups: Berger says there is a special excitement about sociology. Summarize what he means by this statement.

2. In groups: Determine what Berger means by this statement: "The experience of sociological discovery could be described as 'culture shock' minus geographical displacement."

3. For the day this article is due: Students can bring to class a 1-2 page paper on why they are taking this introductory course in sociology--why they signed up for the class and what they expect to get out of it. They can relate their expectations to Berger's article, although this may shape the written role playing into too idealistic a level.

Article 2: Henslin, "Sociology and the Social Sciences"

1. In small groups: Discuss what the author means by his concluding statement: "And, in this enticing process, we have the added pleasure of constantly discovering and rediscovering ourselves."

2. In small groups: Determine what the differences are between the "two types" of sociology.
   (This exercise is designed to pinpoint the students' understandings and misunderstandings, so you can clarify matters in the ensuing discussion and mini-lecture.)

3. In small groups: Discuss what is meant by the statement that sociology is an overarching social science. Illustrate the meaning of this statement.

4. In small groups: Which of the other social sciences comes the closest to sociology? What makes it the closest?

Article 3: Mills, "The Promise"

1. In small groups: Determine how "values" underlie public issues and personal troubles. To do this, you must determine what Mills means by these terms: well-being, crisis, panic, indifference, apathy, uneasiness, and total malaise.
   Note: Students tend to miss the relationship between these terms, yet Mills is presenting a fascinatingly consistent logic. I have found that it clarifies Mills's reasoning to diagram the relationships on the blackboard. I title the diagram "Values and the Sociological Imagination." On the left side I write "Values Cherished" along with the subheadings "Supported" and "Threatened." Under "Supported" I write "Well-Being." Under "Threatened" come the subheadings "Some" (with the subentry "Crisis") and "All" (with the subentry "Panic"). I head the right side of the diagram "Values Not Cherished," again with the subheadings "Supported" and "Threatened." Under "Supported" I add

the subheadings "Some" (with the entry "Indifference") and "All" (with the entry "Apathy"). Under "Threatened" come the subheadings "Some" (with the entries "Uneasiness" and "Anxiety") and "All" (with the entry "Total Malaise").

2. In small groups: Focus on this problem. When Mills discusses "personal troubles" and "public issues," he stresses what he calls "personal experience" and "structural fact." What does he mean by these four terms? How do personal experience and structural fact explain or relate to personal troubles and public issues?

3. In small groups: Discuss why people experience a sense of being trapped. How might the "quality of mind" that Mills calls "the sociological imagination" enable people to get over their sense of being trapped--or at least to better understand it? Do you think people are better off with such understanding, or better off without it? Is "ignorance bliss"?

4. In small groups: Discuss what Mills means when he says, "The sociological imagination enables us to grasp history and biography and the relations between the two within society."

5. In small groups: Discuss what Mills means by his concluding statement that "the sociological imagination is our most needed quality of mind"? Can such an unqualified, universalistic statement possibly be true?

Article 4: Henslin, "How Sociologists Do Research"

1. The class can be given a list of topics, or research questions, that can be answered by consulting Statistical Abstract of the United States. There should be enough topics so each student (or research group) has a different one.

   A large number of questions lend themselves well for this exercise. Examples are: Which American city has the highest crime rate? How does our infant mortality rate compare with what it was ten years ago? How do racial groups compare in terms of number of days sick per year? What proportion of the country's income goes to the richest fifth? What proportion of blacks, whites, and Hispanics are poor?

   Students should be asked to bring to class a photocopy of the table on which they found their answers, and to be able to demonstrate that their conclusions are correct.

2. Students can be given a list of research problems and be asked to show how the various research methods could be applied to solve them. Examples: Does unwed motherhood cause poverty, or does poverty cause unwed motherhood? Does education really lead to higher incomes, or is it that the more intelligent persons, who would have made more money anyway, go on to college?

3. In groups: What are the advantages and disadvantages of quantitative and qualitative research methods?

4. In groups: What is the difference between common sense and sociology? Why is common sense inadequate?

Article 5: Scully and Marolla, "Riding the Bull at Gilley's"

1. For the day this article is due, students can be asked to develop
    an interview schedule designed to uncover how rapists view rape.
    In class, students can share their work in small groups, with each
    small group selecting the interview schedule that it thinks is
    best. The groups can then explain why they made their selections,
    and give examples of questions that they think are very good, as
    well as questions they have now decided are not good.

2. The groups can use the individual interview schedules (they
    developed for the exercise above) to develop a group-based product
    that they turn in for grading.

3. If number 2 is followed, each group can critique another group's
    interview schedule. This works best if no group knows the origin
    of the interview schedule it is critiquing. Each group can then
    read and discuss what it has chosen as the best and worst
    questions.

4. In groups:
    a. Based on this article, just why do men rape?
    b. Knowing these motivations, how could you use this knowledge
        to reduce rape?

5. On rare occasions, I have had class members willing to discuss
    their rape with the class. Much more frequently, however, they
    have been willing to write about their experiences. Occasionally,
    parts of those experiences can be shared with the class. This
    requires that no information be given that might identify the
    victim--and that the individual consent to your sharing the
    particular information.

6. In groups: Assume that you are the governor of your state and
    that you have just been awarded a $25 million grant to reduce
    rape. Based on the information contained in this article, what
    steps should you take?

7. In groups: First, contrast the sociological and psychopathologi-
    cal views of rape; then identify the implications of each view.

Article 6: Chagnon, "Doing Fieldwork Among the Yanomamo"

1. In small groups: Compare your own cultural traits with those of
    the Yanomamo. To do this, draw a parallel list. For example:

    American   Yanomamo
    use tissue or handkerchief   let mucous dribble from nose

2. In small groups or general discussion: What would it be like to
    be a Yanomamo child? How would you be socialized? What would you
    learn?
        To raise awareness about the power of socialization, you may
    wish to have the female students take the role of a Yanomamo boy,
    the male students that of a Yanomamo girl.

23

3. In small groups or general discussion: We find many things strange about the Yanomamo. What might a Yanomamo find strange about our culture? Why do you think that our cultures are so different?

Article 7: Miner, "Body Ritual Among the Nacirema"

1. It is my experience in introducing culture by means of this article that many students who read the article do not grasp the fact that Miner is describing their own culture. Because of this "gradual realization," I sometimes find it instructive to not assign the article, but instead to have it read aloud in class. I have students alternate reading paragraphs aloud, and during the transition between readers I comment on how bizarre that culture is, how it must be very difficult to live there, etc. As this process continues, a light bulb seems to turn on in various parts of the room, giving me a good idea of how this essential fact is being approached.

   At some point, most students understand. I then switch to talking about culture itself, its sweeping role in shaping our behavior, perceptions, attitudes, etc.

   I sometimes use this exercise for the opening class session.

2. In small groups: This humorous article was written in 1956. Because cultures are not static, and the Nacirema culture prides itself on social change, handle this problem: If you were to update this article, what changes would you make?

   After 20-30 minutes, regroup to compare the various "solutions."

3. In small groups: Assume that you were raised in an entirely different culture. You have now arrived in Nacirema and have no knowledge about their life. What practices of the Nacirema might appear strange or bizarre? Why would they appear that way? Why don't they appear strange to the Nacirema?

4. For the day this article is due: Students can bring to class at least one example of a bizarre custom of the Nacirema. They should also write a paragraph in which they explain why this custom is strange. (Examples can be anything from a high-heeled shoe to an advertisement.)

5. In small groups: This role playing provides an interesting exercise in culture. Have the group assume the role of complete strangers to the United States and to the Western World. Although they are unfamiliar with our customs, these people are well educated and speak good English. They are still present in their own culture.

   One of the students has come to them to explain American life in such a way that these people will get along well when they arrive on our shores. They will not be part of a tour group when they arrive here, but will be traveling freely.

6. As a variant, I find it useful to ask each group to draw up a list of "the main characteristics of Americans" that they would tell

24

someone who knew nothing about Americans. When we "regroup," I
keep the students in their individual groups and ask each group to
read what it has listed first. (They have not been told to
prioritize the list.) I then list each characteristic on the
blackboard. I comment on each characteristic, assuming the role
of a tribal member and comparing them to the customs of my tribe.
The resulting list makes a rather strange collection of traits--so
much so that I wonder if I would really like to visit the United
States.

Article 8: Caplow, "The American Way of Celebrating Christmas"

1. In groups: Describe how you celebrate Christmas (or Hanukkah) and
   compare your customs with Caplow's findings. Be ready to report
   to the class your comparisons regarding Christmas decorations,
   Christmas trees, and gift-giving.

2. Each student can bring to class a Christmas advertisement, along
   with a one-page analysis showing the relationship of the ad to
   this article.

3. In groups: Caplow says that the rules about the fitness of gifts
   "are too numerous to specify." Identify some of the rules that
   underlie your evaluations regarding the fitness of gifts.

4. In groups, use your experiences to provide examples of reciprocity
   in gift-giving. Do the findings from Middletown need to be
   modified, or do they dovetail perfectly with your experiences?

5. For the day this article is due, students can interview their
   parents on how they celebrated Christmas when they were children.
   If the grandparents are available, they should interview them
   instead. Each student can bring to class a short paper in which
   he or she compares the family's present Christmas customs with
   those of the parents or grandparents.

Article 9: Goffman, "The Presentation of Self in Everyday Life"

1. In small groups: In his introduction to this article, Henslin
   specifies a direct connection between everyday life and the
   theater. Identify terms from the theater that he does not
   mention, and locate their counterparts in everyday life.

2. As general class discussion or in small groups: If everyday life
   is like the stage, then all of us are actors--as this article
   points out. But if this is true, then where is the "real me"? If
   we all are actors in our daily life, then is everyday life really
   anything more than a "put-on"? Is nothing "real" or "genuine"?
   Where is sincerity?--other than meaning the lines we deliver and
   believing the parts we play? Is there, perhaps, nothing more to
   sincerity than that? Is there, indeed, such a thing as the "real
   me"?

3. In small groups: What does Goffman mean by the term "definition
   of the situation"? Use this article to explain how we develop a
   definition of the situation when we first meet someone. How do

definitions of the situation affect everyday interaction?

4. In small groups: Think about some situation where your definition
    of the situation differed greatly from someone else's. What
    happened? How did the differing definitions affect the
    interaction? How did you resolve the matter (that is, whose
    definitions changed, how did they change, and what were the
    consequences)?

5. In small groups: Discuss instances of people projecting one
    definition of themselves in one situation and a quite different
    definition in other situations.
       The examples students come up with can be fascinating. They
    likely will contrast behavior in the presence of opposite-sexed
    peers, same-sexed peers, parents, and other authority figures.

6. In small groups: In his next to last paragraph, Goffman talks
    about "social disruptions," times when the projected definition of
    the situation fails, creating anything from embarrassment to
    panic. Discuss such situations that you were involved in, or that
    you are familiar with. Analyze what caused the disruption or
    breakdown and its consequences. Was the interaction "repaired"?
    If so, by what "corrective practices"? If not, why not?

Article 10: Davis, "Extreme Isolation"

1. In small groups: List and discuss the similarities and differ-
    ences between Anna and Isabelle. Focus on their early years of
    isolation, as well as the years following their rescue. Finally,
    theorize about how these differences may have affected their
    respective development.
       (For example, Isabelle was kept in a dark room with her mother,
    while Anna was kept in a dark room by herself. This difference
    may have made Isabelle's accelerated language development
    possible. During these years of isolation, Isabelle and her
    mother may have developed some form of nonverbal language, however
    limited, that gave Isabelle a head start in symbolically
    interpreting the world around her.)

2. In small groups: Discuss what your thought life would be like if
    you did not possess a language with which to think words.
       (Later you can have the students extend the idea of a world
    without words and discuss such issues as: What would life be like
    if no one could speak? How could one ever make plans? How
    developed could society ever become?)
       During this exercise, presenting materials on Helen Keller is
    enlightening for the students. Most introductory texts feature
    her thought development.

3. In small groups: Try to relate this reading to the nature of
    human nature. That is, what are we without language? What would
    our behavior be like? How would one's self-concept be different?
    Could we even possess a self-concept?
       You may wish to have the students list on the left side of a
    piece of paper the precise point in the article (with page number)
    they are drawing from, and, on the right, the conclusion

concerning human nature that they infer from this point. This will keep the discussion on track as they look for inferences. The after-group discussion period can both examine the idea of human nature and the logic of the students' inferences.

4. In small groups: Discuss what Davis means by his concluding statement: "...only in these rare cases of extreme isolation is it possible to observe concretely separated two factors in the development of human personality which are always otherwise only analytically separated, the biogenic and sociogenic factors"?

Article 11: Henslin, "On Becoming Male"

1. For the day this article is due, students can write a short paper in which they compare their childhood socialization with that depicted in this reading. The assignment can be left this general, or specific areas can be delineated, e.g., socialization into sexuality, into orientation toward members of the other sex, into self-concept, into life aspirations, etc.
    You are to explore the social factors that shaped you into the kind of male or female that you now are. That is, you are attempting to answer the same question as the author grapples with: "What is the social origin of your gender orientation?"

2. In small groups: What was the significance of play in your becoming masculine or feminine? Compare your childhood play with that discussed in this article.

3. In small groups: Why are sports, including their televised versions, so important to so many males? Why, on average, are they less important to females? Tie your answer directly into this reading.

4. In small groups: Why are intersexual interactions generally so superficial? That is, use the materials in this article to explain why so many males have such a difficult time to really care about a female's activities, but instead seem to concentrate their efforts on obtaining sexual favors?

5. In small groups: How might you socialize your male children so they are less sexist?

Article 12: Thorne and Luria, "Sexuality and Gender"

1. In groups: The authors mention several sex-segregated childhood games and activities. Think about when you were a child. What sex-segregated games or activities not mentioned in this article did you participate in? Why do you think children of this age are so careful to draw firm lines between the sexes?

2. For the day this article is due, students can report on their observations of children's play. Recess in grade school is especially appropriate.

3. Grade school children can be invited to form a panel to discuss what they think of the opposite sex. Their favorite games and

27

playmates can then become a topic of discussion.

4. The class can draw up a list of questions pertaining to sex-segregated preferences and activities of children. Students can tape interviews with their younger brothers and sisters, or with neighborhood children, and compare their findings with those of Thorne and Luria. The taping is suggested because the most interesting tapes can be played for the class.

5. In groups: Take a position on this statement: "The everyday worlds of boys and girls are a microcosm of the adult world." Be specific, and be ready to support your position.

Article 13: Henley, Hamilton, and Thorne, "Womanspeak and Manspeak"

1. In small groups: Draw up a list of sexist sayings or quotations (which you will share with the class). Why do you think those sayings are part of our culture?

2. For the day this article is due, each student can bring to class sexist lyrics from two different songs. Students should also write a paragraph about each lyric, indicating how it relates to the article.

3. The class can be divided into male-only and female-only groups to discuss: "What I like about females (males)." You can write the groups' conclusions on the blackboard (preferably remaining straight-faced). Afterwards, you can indicate the sexist assumptions of some of the observations.

4. In small groups: Draw up a list of terms for women who have a lot of sexual partners. Do the same for men.
   When the entire class reconvenes, you can list on the black-board all the terms the groups have come up with. How close did they come to the 10 times more terms for females that the authors report? Is there any indication from this that attitudes are changing? Did the students' lists include any positive terms (e.g., virile, strong, potent)? If so, are they evenly divided between men and women? If not...

5. In small groups: When the authors say that "there are differences between female and male speech styles," they are referring to both verbal and nonverbal communication. Provide examples of differences in verbal and nonverbal communication that are not mentioned in the article.

Article 14: Snyder, "Self-Fulfilling Stereotypes"

1. In groups: Stereotypes are part of everyday life, and, as this article points out, they can have far-reaching effects. I would like you to examine your own life in terms of stereotypes or labels. Specifically, what labels were placed on you that influenced your development? (For example, clumsy, graceful, athletic, strong, weak, smart, dumb?) What effects did they have?

2. In groups: The author makes this statement: "I suspect that even

if people were to develop doubts about the accuracy of their stereotypes, chances are they would proceed to test them by gathering precisely the evidence that would appear to confirm them." Are there any situations in which you have seen this happen?

3. In groups: Identify common stereotypes in American life that are not covered in this article. Discuss their effects on people and organizations.

4. In groups: One way that groups increase their solidarity is to compare themselves to out-groups, persons presumed to have highly undesirable traits. First, identify such out-groups and the stereotypes used to characterize them. You are encouraged to draw on your own experiences in groups--including grade school and high school. Because not all stereotypes are negative, your second task is to identify the stereotypes that characterized your own members. Finally, try to identify the effects of these stereotypes.

5. In groups: What evidence does the author offer to support his statement: "Stereotypes are not merely beliefs or attitudes that exist in a vacuum; they are reinforced by the behavior of both prejudiced people and the targets of their prejudice"?

6. In groups: What does this statement from the introduction to the article mean: "Stereotypes socially reproduce their imagery"? What evidence can you find in the article to support this statement?

Article 15: Whyte, "Street People"

1. In groups: Of what value is the type of information contained in this article?

2. For the day this article is due, students can prepare a paper in which they compare their own systematic observations at some location (bus stop, cafeteria, classroom, soda machine, etc.) with those of Whyte. It may be advisable to make Whyte's book available to the class as it contains detailed observations on many different types of interactions.

3. Students can also record the seating arrangements in some class in which seats are not assigned. (They can record sex, race, age, or any variables they choose.) The "maps" (see the entry on Whyte in the section on "About the Contributors" in the text) that the students bring to class can then be compared to see if any factors seem to hold constant.

4. An interesting variant of number 3 is to ask the students to chart the seating arrangement of a class and to record who volunteers questions and answers. The number of times each person does so should be recorded. These charts can then be compared to see if there is greater participation from some parts of the room. If so, the subtlety of social influences on human behavior will become more evident to them.

5.   <u>For the day this article is due</u>: The proliferation of video
cameras in our culture can be turned to a major advantage in the
classroom. One exercise that I have found especially valuable--
and entertaining--is to have students videotape some segment of
urban life, to narrate it, and to show it to the class. I have
found that students are highly creative in what they videotape, in
the music they select as background, and in their narrations.

What is especially enlightening to the class is that the
subject is their own city, and the "local" takes on new meaning as
it is interpreted through camera work and the sociological content
of the article.

Five- and ten-minute video segments are especially effective.
They allow much time for discussion and avoid the students'
getting so caught up in watching a video that they lose sight of
the sociological significance of the assignment.

<u>Article 16</u>. Henslin, "Trust and Cabbies"

1. In small groups: Discuss a situation in which you did not trust a
stranger or someone whom you did not know very well. What made
you feel that way? Relate your feelings of distrust to the
article, tying into stereotypes that lead to trust and distrust.

2. In small groups: Analyze a situation in which you trusted someone
you shouldn't have. Why did you trust that person? Relate your
feelings of trust to the article, tying into stereotypes that lead
to trust and distrust. How did this event change your perception
of whom you can trust?

3. In small groups: Try to combine this article with the one by
Snyder (number 14). In what ways does Snyder's analysis help
interpret Henslin's findings?

4. <u>For the day this article is due</u>, students can write a paper in
which they compare their own experiences of trust and distrust
with those reported here. They can be encouraged to explore their
own stereotypes that influence their perception.

<u>Article 17</u>: Clark, "Sympathy in Everyday Life"

1. Although the following lends itself well either for small group
discussions or as a paper to be prepared outside of class, many
students will need a lot of guidance with this assignment. The
potential it holds for opening their perceptions into this aspect
of life in society, however, can make this exercise highly
rewarding.

Use Clark's article to illustrate this statement: "Sociology
has a subfield called 'the sociology of emotions.' Sociologists
who work in this area stress that emotions are 'socially
patterned'; that is, emotions are not simply spontaneous feelings,
but they change according to culture and according to membership
in different groups within a society. This principle applies both
to how we <u>express</u> emotions and to <u>what</u> <u>we</u> <u>feel</u>."

2. Clark makes an interesting point about how some people "bankrupt

30

their sympathy accounts." Provide examples from your own
experience.

3. In small groups, analyze a situation in which:
    a. someone did not give you the sympathy that you felt you
        deserved;
    b. you "gave" sympathy, but you felt that you really shouldn't
        have had to give it;
    c. you manipulated others into giving sympathy.
    In each instance, relate your experiences to Clark's research.

4. In small groups: Discuss the five rules of sympathy etiquette.
    Provide examples of each from your own experience. Based on your
    own experience, try to identify other rules of sympathy etiquette.

Article 18: Henslin and Biggs, "Vaginal Examination"

1. A feminist sociologist wrote to me that she likes to use Down to
    Earth Sociology, but is too timid to use this article. She was
    apologetic because she liked the article but felt uncomfortable
    discussing this topic in mixed classes. If you are uncomfortable,
    skip the class discussion. I encourage you to use it in the
    classroom, however, because it does work. The students are
    interested in the topic, and it allows them to better see the
    social construction of reality.

2. The following letter to Ann Landers can serve as the basis for
    small group or class discussions. Due to copyright, I shall
    paraphrase the letter.
        Dear Annie: I just found out what the father of our new next
    door neighbor does, and I am shocked. He is a medical doctor, and
    he treats his three daughters when they are sick. That doesn't
    bother me, but I also found out that he gives them their vaginal
    examinations and pap smears!
        Isn't their a law against this? Do most doctors do this? Why
    do you think their mother allows it? Don't you think this is
    sexual abuse? Should I call the hot line?--Shocked in Peoria
        Dear Shocked: You aren't too far off. The physicians I
    checked with said it was okay to treat your daughters when they
    are ill, but to give them vaginal examinations is unprofessional.
    One even described this practice as sick.

3. A feminist (or a representative from the Women's Center or Women's
    Studies) can address the class on such issues as the control by
    men over women's bodies, the objectification of women by the
    medical establishment and in society in general, the demeaning
    aspects of medical treatment, sexual exploitation, and solutions
    to these problems. You may want to give the guest a copy of this
    article in advance of the presentation.

4. On occasion, the class contains students whose background allows
    them to more freely discuss matters such as their own vaginal
    examinations. On occasion also, some students (or someone they
    know) have been sexually exploited by physicians during medical
    treatment (not necessarily vaginal examinations). If these
    experiences are shared, the failure to desexualize during medical

procedures can be explored.

5. Female students can explore the relationship between the "self"
   and the vaginal examination. They might recount their first
   vaginal examination and analyze what happened to their fears and
   anxieties. Do they now fully accept the definition of
   nonsexuality? How have their ideas changed? How did that
   transition occur? How do they feel about vaginal examinations?
   Why do so many women put off having vaginal examinations?
       Based on my experience, all-female groups provide greater
   freedom of exchange on this topic. If the groups are arranged
   this way, males can either focus on a different article, or they
   can discuss anxieties they may have experienced in medical
   situations, such as the common one of the doctor saying, "Drop
   your pants," while the male patient is in the presence of a female
   nurse.
       It also is my experience that following these small-group
   discussions females quite readily share their observations with
   the entire class. For feelings of solidarity, I have found that
   this is best done while the students are still seated in their
   small groups.

6. As I have explored this topic with my classes, I have found that,
   when probed more deeply, their is a deep-seated feeling that the
   vaginal examination is not entirely asexual. Exploring these
   feelings makes for an enlightening class discussion. The letter
   to Ann Landers in exercise 1 is relevant for this topic.

7. In small groups: Discuss how this article relates to Goffman's
   article (number 9).

Article 19: Schwartz, "Waiting, Exchange, and Power"

1. In small groups: Analyze the following event in terms of this
   article.
       After a stimulating class, a professor and a student were
   walking down the hallway talking about what had happened in class.
   Just as the student was making a point, the professor spotted a
   colleague, walked over to her and asked about the outcome of the
   meeting on the appropriations for a new departmental computer.
   The student waited at the sidelines. In a couple of minutes the
   professor rejoined the student, muttered something about budget
   problems, and then began talking about the events in class.
       Later, you might ask the class how the interaction would have
   been different if the professor had been walking with the
   president of the college or university and had seen the same
   colleague.

2. In papers, groups, or class discussions: Analyze an instance of
   "prolonged waiting" that you have experienced. Use Schwartz's
   analysis of waiting and power to explain the instance, including
   your feelings and actions.

3. In small groups: Relate this material to some situation in your
   own life in which there was an imbalance in waiting. Interpret
   this imbalance in terms of the interpersonal power of that

relationship.

Article 20: Thompson, "Hanging Tongues"

1. For the day this article is due, students who have worked on
    assembly lines can write a short paper in which they compare their
    experiences with those reported in this article. If there are
    sufficient numbers of such students, they also can serve as a
    panel. They can be asked to focus on the setting, the work
    itself, the worker's lack of control, and the basic coping
    strategies of the workers.

2. In small groups: Compare your own work experiences with those
    reported by Thompson. The basic foci can be the status of the
    job, its routines, the worker's sense of control (or lack
    thereof), basic problems at work, and basic coping strategies.
    The groups can be formed as usual, or those who have worked at
    demanding and demeaning jobs can be asked to form separate groups.

3. In small groups: The author discusses formal and informal norms,
    e.g., the formal norm of placing dropped meat into tubs marked
    inedible versus the informal norm of covertly placing the meat
    back on the assembly line. What other contrasts between formal
    and informal norms can you locate in this article? Compare those
    with the formal and informal norms you have followed at work. As
    you do this, try to develop an explanation for why the informal
    norm exists (as Thompson does for the example above).
        Note: With students' occupational experiences being so varied,
    this exercise works very well. Frankly, I have been rather
    surprised at some of the informal norms that students have
    reported. Some have even changed my perceptions--especially my
    discovering that one of the ushers at a local theater takes his
    shoes and socks off and cools his feet in the ice machine from
    which the ice is taken for the soft drinks!

4. In small groups: It appears that workers in all occupational
    settings develop informal "games" that they play with one another.
    As in this article, some of these games involve "the subtle art of
    rule-breaking." Others are of a different nature. Based on your
    own occupational experiences, identify and discuss both types.

Article 21: Coleman, "Diary of a Homeless Man"

1. For the day this article is due, students can report on the
    assistance available to the homeless in their local communities.
    They can bring to class a list of what they found plus a one-page
    summary of how they think such assistance could be practically
    improved. When the class meets as a whole, you can use the
    blackboard to summarize their conclusions.

2. For the day this article is due, students can bring to class a
    one- to two-page essay on "How the problem of homelessness can be
    solved." In small groups, students can share their analyses with
    one another. When the class meets as a whole to summarize its
    conclusions, you can use the blackboard to divide their opinions
    into institutional and individual.

This exercise, designed to help students develop their sociological imagination, should help them better perceive institutionally rooted causes of homelessness, possible institutional responses if homelessness is to be solved, and the interconnectedness of our social institutions.

3. Students are very resourceful, and one or two may be interested in repeating Coleman's experience. If so, they can write a term paper in which they draw direct comparisons between their experiences on the streets, those of Coleman, and literature on the topic. If the papers are due before the term is over, they can be shared in class.

4. For the day this article is due, students can interview a homeless person and relate their findings to those reported by Coleman. These can be shared in the small group format.

    In making this assignment, I have found that students are frightened at the prospect of talking to homeless people. First, they need reassurance that these are people. Second, they need to know that they are not being asked to talk to strangers in alleys at midnight. I find it helpful to tell them that the interviews should be done in daylight in public settings, such as shelters or busy streets.

5. For the day this article is due, students can bring to class a one- to two-page paper in which they compare Coleman's observations with analyses of various forms of discrimination. Examples would be articles by Benokraitis and Feagin, Chambliss, Fields, Hughes, Liebow, and Murray in this text.

6. In small groups: How do Coleman's observations relate to the materials presented in the articles by (list one: Benokraitis and Feagin, Chambliss, Fields, Hughes, Liebow, or Murray)?

Article 22: Henslin, "The Survivors of the F-227"

1. In small groups: Discuss the ethics of eating human flesh for survival.

2. Take a poll of the class. How many would eat others for survival? Why or why not?

    Would you do so under the circumstances outlined in this article?

    Would you do so if you were quite sure that help was coming in 30 days, but you couldn't be positive?

    Would you do so if for some reason you had access to a meat grinder, other members of the group prepared the meat, and it would be available as cooked hamburger on buns?

    Would you do so if your life depended on it and, somehow, the meat came from the corpse of _____? (Fill in with the current "big, bad guy" of the United States. As I write this, it is Saddam Hussein, but these political enemies are ever changing.)

3. In groups: Why do humans develop norms?

Article 23. Chambliss, "The Saints and the Roughnecks"

1. Youth workers (social workers, police, or religious) can be contacted to present their perspective on their work with delinquents to the class.

2. In small groups: The main theme running through this article is that labels, given to teenagers, open and close doors of opportunity and have lifelong effects. Discuss how labeling influenced the lives of these youngsters. Then from your own experiences, relate how labeling has affected either yourself or someone you know.

3. In small groups: Compare your own "escapades" during high school with those of the "Saints" and the "Roughnecks." In what ways did your "reputation" either protect or harm you? (If you wish to compare the activities of others in your high school, rather than those of yourself, you may do so.)

   If, like the high school students in this article, you were heavily involved in illegal acts, how did you end up in college?

4. In small groups: In the last section of this article, Chambliss applies the principle of reinforcement to labeling, the self-concept, and commitment to deviance or commitment to conformity. First explain this principle; then apply it to situations with which you are familiar.

Article 24: Marx, "Unintended Consequences of Undercover Work"

1. Your local police department can be asked to send a detective to make a presentation on undercover work to the class.

2. In groups: What factors lead an individual to cross over to the other side? Be sociological in your analysis. That is, do not come up with "personality" or "idiosyncrasies" of any sort as an answer. Look for group-based causes.

3. In groups: How influential is role playing in our lives? Consider the implications of this article—that we become the roles we play—whether those are positive or negative roles.

4. In groups: If you were the chief of detectives of a large city, how would you prevent an undercover agent from crossing over to the other side? Be ready to explain the principles (covered in this article) on which your suggestions are based.

Article 25: Zimbardo, "The Pathology of Imprisonment"

1. You can sponsor a field trip to the local jail or the area prison. This needs to be well planned in advance, but the pay-off in understanding this social institution is sometimes worth the effort.

2. A parole officer can serve as a contact for recruiting former prisoners to address the class on the treatment they received.

3. Workers in jails and prisons, as well as judges, are sometimes

willing to address a college class on their role and experiences. You may wish to send the speaker or panel members a copy of this article in advance.

4. In small groups: Zimbardo's experiment demonstrates that the social structure of prisons underlies prison violence. Based on this article, how do you think prisons might be reconstructed in order to minimize violence.

5. In small groups: A common attitude in our society is, "Because tough people are sent to prisons, prisons need to be tough. The tougher prisons are, the better it is for society." What evidence does the Zimbardo experiment provide for or against this argument?

6. In small groups: How can a prison be "tough," without being violent? That is, there is a public outcry against giving light sentences to offenders. Can they be sent to a prison that will satisfy the public's demand for being "tough" with the goal of rehabilitation?

7. In small groups: Discuss the proposals that Zimbardo makes for prison reform. How do you think they could be implemented?

Article 26: Rosenhan, "On Being Sane in Insane Places"

1. For the day this article is due, invite mental health workers to serve as a panel. Their primary purpose can be to respond to student questions based on this article. In fairness, panel members should be sent a copy of the article in advance so they can anticipate the students' questions.
    To get the panel started, each member can introduce himself or herself and summarize his or her job description.

2. A field trip is highly applicable for this reading. Although you will have to make advance arrangements, a visit to a mental hospital can be worth more than reading a dozen articles about these institutions.

3. A la Garfinkel, students can be asked to engage in neurotic, compulsive behavior in public places. Examples might be to continuously pick one's nose, to talk aloud to oneself while staring into space, etc. A confederate or two should be present to observe the reactions of bystanders--as well as to give support in case something untoward should occur.
    These observations can be written up as a group project. In the paper students can relate their findings both to this article and to others in this part of the book.

4. In small groups: Explain how the psychiatric diagnosis (a form of labeling) affects perception. In what ways is this similar to Chambliss's findings on labeling as reported in his study of the Saints and the Roughnecks (article 23)?

5. In small groups: When the personnel of one hospital found out about this experiment, they said that nothing like that could ever happen in their hospital. Rosenhan said that he would have a

36

pseudopatient admitted to their hospital within the next three months. What happened? Specify precisely how that could happen.

6. How could you use the article by Snyder (number 14) to help interpret Rosenhan's findings.

Article 27: Domhoff, "The Bohemian Grove and Other Retreats"

1. In small groups: A controversial point runs through this selection, namely, Domhoff's hypothesis that there is a ruling class in the United States. As Domhoff says, most social scientists disagree with this view.
    Discuss Domhoff's position. Evaluate the evidence that Domhoff presents. Do you agree with Domhoff that there is a national upper class? Why or why not?

2. A term project could be a study of your area's local elite. Early in the term, students can be assigned the task of gathering information on local politicians, especially their family background, connection with area businesses, and wealth/income.
    With guidance, this project can result in highly informative, "real-life" materials that illustrate gender, wealth, ethnic, and age distinctions in community power.

3. In groups: Determine the social significance of the Bohemian Grove (and other retreats).

4. In groups: Outline the evidence that Domhoff uses to develop his thesis that a national upper class governs the United States.

5. In groups: Contrast the pluralist view of the power structure of the United States with that presented by Domhoff.

Article 28: Gans, "The Uses of Poverty"

1. In groups: Review the 13 functions of poverty that Gans presents. In your opinion, are any of these items not really functions of poverty? If so, why not? Try to determine functions that Gans may have overlooked.

2. In groups or general class discussion: The main point of this selection is that the poor are present in society because they perform valuable functions for society. Do you agree with this hypothesis? If this position is true, is it, then, impossible to get rid of poverty? To eradicate poverty would require that we find alternatives to each of the functions that the poor now perform for society. Evaluate the alternatives that Gans discusses. What alternatives would you add?

3. In groups: If the poor perform such valuable services for society, why is there such widespread resentment by the middle class against the poor in our society?

4. In groups: Based on this article, how can we eliminate poverty? Be specific.

Article 29: Benokraitis and Feagin, "Sex Discrimination"

1. You can divide the class into all-male and all-female groups. The
    females can discuss ways that they have experienced discrimination
    on the basis of their sex, while the males discuss ways that they
    have discriminated against females (or ways they, too, have been
    discriminated against).
        After each group has shared its experiences with the class, the
    students can break into groups made up of both males and females
    and discuss their experiences.

2. For the day this article is due, students can bring to class
    advertisements that they think illustrate sex discrimination--
    along with a one-page analysis of what is discriminatory about the
    ad. Having the students share the ads and their analyses with the
    class makes for a lively exchange of perspectives.

3. You can bring to class copies of tables from Statistical Abstract
    of the United States and ask the students, in groups, to discern
    the sex bias. Ask each group to write one or two paragraphs, to
    be shared with the class, in which they analyze the discrimination
    that they discern. Tables on income, occupation, and property
    lend themselves well for this purpose.

4. In groups, discuss whether female reporters should be allowed in
    male locker rooms after a game.

Article 30: Fields and Fields, "The School at Society Corner"

1. In small groups: Contrast the ways that blacks and whites were
    treated in this school system.

2. In small groups: Why was such inequality allowed? Keep in mind
    that the people who practiced this inequality believed in the
    United States Constitution that declares "All men are created
    equal."

3. In small groups: Try to determine how the racial inequality in
    public schools at the time these events took place was related to
    racial inequality in other aspects of society.
        The class's attempts to handle this topic will expose their
    gaps in knowledge about the structured social inequality of that
    period. In addition to filling those gaps, you will also have the
    opportunity to apply the concept of structured social inequality
    to our contemporary society (such as discrimination in employment
    and the ghetto itself), showing students that this article is more
    than interesting history.

4. In small groups: Segregated schools like this one are a thing of
    the past. Yet we still face racial segregation in many areas of
    life in American society. Identify those segregated areas and
    identify how, like the School at Society Corner, they are
    functional for some parts of society. (That is, who benefits from
    the segregation you have identified?)

Article 31: Liebow, "Tally's Corner"

1. In small groups: A central theme running through this article is that negative self-images destroy initiative and aspiration and lock people into failure. Trace this theme. Analyze the specific examples Liebow presents in terms of the consequences of negative self-images. Also try to identify the sources of such self-images.

2. In small groups: Explain how Snyder's article (number 14) is relevant to this article.

3. In small groups: A new President of the United States has just been elected, and for your help in swinging the Moravian vote to his side, you have been appointed Director of USAID, the United States Agency for Internal Development. Your main goal for the next four years is to change the lives of streetcorner men and women. What are you going to do?

   After the students have developed their program and together with the class you have evaluated their practicality and value, you may wish to direct the discussion to: (a) What values underlie the changes that you want to bring about? (b) What is the "image" you are following, and why do you wish to change people to match that particular "image"? (c) Should the federal government have anything to do with trying to change people, even though its intentions may be good?

4. Review the concept of the self-fulfilling prophecy with the class. In groups: Discuss this concept, identify how the self-fulfilling prophecy operates in the lives of these streetcorner men, and recount examples of how it has worked in your own life.

Article 32: Hughes, "Good People and Dirty Work"

1. In small groups: Some experts say that the Nazis were able to get by with their programs of terror and genocide because the Germans have a strong tendency to accept authority. Others say it was because of Germany's social structure (how the society was organized). Take a side, and develop an argument for that side.

   After discussion, each group can choose the side it wishes to take and a debate can be held. The main value, of course, comes from contrasting individualistic and structuralistic reasoning.

2. Now that Germany is reunited, it appears destined to become the powerhouse of Europe. Its standard of living already rivals that of the United States, and is likely to surpass ours soon. In the past, whenever the Germans became powerful, they attacked their neighbors and tried to dominate Europe. Why should we be certain that they will be satisfied with economic dominance this time? What can we do to prevent them from waging another war?

3. Anti-Semitism has not ceased to exist in Germany. Now that their goal of unification has been achieved, what is to prevent persons with the neo-Nazi and skinhead mentalities from gaining power and embarking on another Holocaust?

4. For class discussion: Some say that the Nazis were an aberration

on the pages of history, that what happened in Germany was due to
a unique configuration of historical events, that such conditions
never will be repeated. Therefore, we need have no fear that such
an event will ever occur in our midst.

Others say that Nazism never did die--the ideas simply went
underground where they have been germinating. When the time is
again ripe, during a period of social disturbance and economic
upheaval, Nazis again will spring forth full-blown.

What do you think? What indications are there on the current
historical scene to support either view?

5. In small groups: Determine the circumstances that would be needed
   for a Holocaust to happen in the United States.

Article 33: Gracey, "Learning the Student Role"

1. In small groups, students can discuss:
   a. the benefits to schools and society of having children learn
      the student role--conforming, lining up, following
      directions, not interrupting;
   b. the costs or negative consequences of learning the student
      role; and,
   c. what the classroom would be like (including yours) if
      students did not follow the student role.
   d. If, then, learning the student role is necessary, are there
      alternatives to stifling individuality, initiative,
      independence, and creativity?

2. From their own experiences, students can provide examples that are
   not included in the article of how they learned the student role.

3. For the day this article is due, students can observe a kindergarten or preschool and apply their observations to this article.

4. In groups: You are all kindergarten teachers. Devise a classroom
   that works, but that does not have the negative features analyzed
   by Gracey.

Article 34: Roache, "Confessions of a Househusband"

1. A househusband can be invited to speak to the class. I have found
   that students enjoy their presentations and the discussions that
   follow.

2. If any female members of the class would like their husbands to be
   a full-time househusband, they can be asked to explain why. The
   same can be done with male students who would like a full-time
   housewife.

3. Scenes from "Who's the Boss?" can be shown the class, especially
   those that show Tony more effective at household tasks than Angela
   and those that show Tony being defensive about what he does.

Article 35: Roache, "The Myth of Male Helplessness"

1. Students can share "horror stories" about inept husbands who made

40

bizarre mistakes in doing housework or in performing traditionally
female roles around the house. The discussion will indicate
whether they were intended to sabotage attempts at changing their
role or that they only indicate inadequate socialization.

2. Married students can share the specifics of how they divide the
housework with their spouses.

3. For the day this article is due, students can bring to class
examples from the mass media of the perpetuation of the myth of
male helplessness. Full-page color ads and videotapes of
commercials and short scenes from television programs are
especially effective.

4. In small groups: Let us suppose that you are married and that you
dislike housework intensely. You want your spouse to do all the
housework, or at least almost all of it. Outline steps that you
might take to accomplish this. Be practical--and effective.

Article 36: Hong and Dearman, "The Streetcorner Preacher"

1. A streetcorner preacher could be invited as a guest presenter to
explain his role to the class. Contacts can sometimes be made
through local pastors. If streetcorner preachers are unavailable,
evangelistic pastors may be asked to do the same thing. These are
primarily Baptists, Assemblies of God, Salvation Army, and those
listed in the Yellow Pages under the heading "Churches" and the
subheading "Pentecostal" or "Independent."

2. David Wilkerson is a nationally-known street preacher who worked
with gangs in New York City. A video based on his best-selling
book, The Cross and the Switchblade, can be ordered from Vanguard
Video, 4111 South Darlington, suite 600, Tulsa, OK 74135.

3. The epitome of American evangelism is Billy Graham. One of his
videos can be shown in class and analyzed afterwards. Videos
featuring Billy Graham are available from Worldwide Publications,
1303 Hennepin, Minneapolis, MN 55403. These can be ordered
through any video vender or local Bible Bookstore and sometimes
can be borrowed from a local Baptist church.

4. The evangelization techniques used on the electronic media can be
contrasted with those analyzed in this article. Especially
contrastive with the techniques of streetcorner preachers is the
sophisticated approach of the 700 Club, with its primary appeal to
the middle class. Students can be asked to compare this article
with some segment of the 700 Club.

5. In small groups: When the authors began their research, they
appear to have shared the popular assumption that streetcorner
preachers are somewhat unbalanced. After doing their research,
what did they conclude? On what did they base their conclusions?

Article 37: Lyng, "Edgework"

1. If anyone in your class is involved in edgework, that person can

make a presentation—or can simply answer questions from the class.

2. Edgeworkers can be invited to class to share their experiences and perspectives.

3. In groups: Why do edgeworkers do what they do? (What motivates them to take risks that most of us avoid?)

4. In groups: What activities have you engaged in that might be considered a form of edgework?

5. The class can be divided into groups on the basis of those who either have skydived or would like to and those who would refuse to skydive even though they had the opportunity. Those who are not certain what their attitudes are can make up a third type of group. The exchange of perspectives following the small group discussion can be enlightening for the students.

Article 38: Haas and Shaffir, "The Cloak of Competence"

1. For the day this article is due, students can bring to class examples from the popular literature that illustrate the "expectation of competence" surrounding physicians. This can be competence expected either by the public or by the physicians themselves. Medical advertisements lend themselves well for this purpose.
   Along with the illustration, each student can bring a written statement in which he or she explains (a) how the choice illustrates either the expectation or display of competence; and (b) through specific tie-ins with the reading, how the reading helps to explain the illustration.
   Students can share their analyses with one another in small groups, with each group selecting one (or two) papers that in their opinion provide the best illustration. These choices can then be shared with the class as a whole.

2. In small groups: Discuss this common dilemma: "How can I determine that my doctor is competent?" You must distinguish between competence and the "cloak" of competence.

3. Divide the class into groups. Have half the groups prepare for a debate-discussion on this topic, "It is good for doctors to present an all-knowing facade," while the other groups prepare to take this position, "Doctors should do less role-playing and be more honest—and that includes letting patients know their limitations of medical expertise."

4. In small groups: How would you restructure medical training in order to produce physicians who are more "patient oriented," that is, doctors who are more concerned with the entire welfare of the patient rather than merely the course of his or her illness?

Article 39: Hunt, "Police Accounts of Normal Force"

1. If possible, have a female police officer make a presentation to the class. The class can then ask her about her socialization

into the use of force.

2. In small groups:
   a. Determine the differences between accounts, excuses, and justifications. How are they used by the police?
   b. How are they used by people in everyday life? Provide examples from your own life.
   c. Now analyze the role of accounts, excuses, and justifications in everyday life.

3. In small groups: Analyze why the police tend to be violent beyond that which is permitted by law. Identify the various factors that encourage and perpetuate the use of illegal force.

   After the students have clearly established the processes, they can wrestle with these two issues: (a) If I were to become a police officer and if I did not want to use illegal force, how could I manage to keep my standards? (b) What changes would one have to make in order to have supervisors and street "cops" provide a subculture that discourages the use of force beyond that provided by law? Be practical.

4. In small groups: A "street cop" regularly comes up against mean, violent people. How is it possible for female "cops" to survive in this environment?

   This exercise uncovers masculine/feminine stereotypes so they can be examined.

Article 40: Mills, "The Structure of Power in American Society"

1. In small groups: Determine what Mills means by the "middle levels of power" in American society. Who occupies those levels? What is the relationship of those occupants to the top and bottom levels of power? Evaluate what Mills says about the different levels of power.

2. In small groups: Assume that Mills's hypothesis is correct. First analyze the future course of democracy in the United States. Then determine possible means, or alternative forms of political organization that might serve to reverse the trend and return power back to smaller groups of citizens.

Article 41: Murray, "The Abolition of El Cortito"

1. A local union can be asked to send a representative to the class. A union organizer would be the preferable course.

2. If there are migrant farm workers in your area, you can check to see if any students have sufficient contacts to interview them or their employers, or even to videotape their working and living conditions.

3. If there are migrant farm workers in your area, you can call your county and state agencies to see who works with them. They may be willing to send a representative to your class. Similarly, a social worker who works with them may make a presentation.

4. In groups: Identify the factors that allowed El Cortito to be
    banned. What specific obstacles had to be overcome? What was the
    source of the conflict between interest groups?

5. In groups: Identify other areas of American society in which
    profits are put ahead of health--whether of workers or of the
    public. Applying the lessons from El Cortito, what steps would
    have to be taken in order to change these practices?

Article 42: Ouchi, "Decision-Making in Japanese Organizations"

1. Small groups (or perhaps the entire class) can be asked to solve a
    problem using the Japanese approach of consensus. This should be
    a problem that involves making a policy decision--a resolution
    that reqires some kind of action.
        A theoretical problem will work, as long as different
    interests, attitudes, or backgrounds are reflected. For example,
    students can role play workers at different positions with varying
    time on the job. Some can have been on the job for only weeks,
    others for many years. Some can be skilled workers, others
    unskilled. Some can be in lower and upper ranks of management.
    All can be told: "You are a member of 'Y' work force, and the
    company can no longer afford for everyone to take two weeks'
    vacation. There is money for only a one-week vacation--if it were
    divided evenly among all workers. Not all workers like this
    solution, however--especially those with the most seniority who,
    after 25 and 30 years on the job, have come to the point that they
    are eligible for five or six weeks' vacation a year."
        After the students have had an opportunity to achieve
    consensus, they can discuss the process by which they arrived at
    consensus--or failed to do so. Following this, they can discuss
    the viability of such an approach in the American setting.

2. The exercise outlined above can also be used with a "real"
    problem, one for which the students will be affected by the
    consequences of their decision. The decision will go into effect
    only if there is consensus.
        Examples are:
    a. Hold out a $20 bill. (A $50 is even better, but...) Tell
        the students that they can do whatever they wish with it as
        long as everyone in the class agrees. Otherwise, you will
        keep it.
    b. Students can be told: "You can decide exactly what kind of
        final examination you will have in this course. It will be
        entirely up to you--as long as everyone agrees. If there
        is even one person who disagrees, the final will be exactly
        as I decide. You cannot use ridicule or other negative
        approaches in getting people to agree. There must be real
        consensus that a particular decision is desirable."
    c. The example in 2b can be changed to include the term paper
        for the course.

Article 43: Zuboff, "New Worlds of Computer-Mediated Work"

1. For the day this article is due, each student can bring an article
    on computers (preferably something on the social dimensions or

44

ramifications of computers, but almost anything will do, except for strictly technical descriptions). In addition, each student should have written a short paper in which he or she draws direct comparisons between the selected article and Zuboff's analysis.

In groups, the students can share their conclusions, and each group can select one paper to be presented to the entire class.

2. In small groups: Discuss whether supervisors ought to be allowed to monitor workers' production without the workers' knowledge.
    Variant: Students can be self-selected into groups on the basis of their taking a pro or con position on: "Supervisors should be allowed to monitor workers' production without the workers' knowledge." Students can then prepare their position and meet on opposing sides for a general debate.

3. In small groups: Employers are demanding an ever increasing control over workers. Computers are one major means of gaining this control. Another issue that is of concern to workers is the right of employers to demand drug tests of their workers. What is your position on mandatory drug-testing in the work place?

4. For the day this article is due, students who have work experience in settings in which information technology is employed can bring in a short paper in which they compare their experiences with those analyzed by Zuboff. They may want to focus on the human reaction to the introduction of computers to the work place, the effects of computers on relations among workers, or to the ways in which computers tend to "take on authority." These papers can be shared with the class.

5. In small groups: Discuss the implications of information techno-logy for human relationships in the work place.

Article 44: Rodriguez, "Searching for Roots in a Changing World"

1. The author has written a book on his experiences entitled The Education of Richard Rodriguez. You can supplement this article by reading to the class selections from this book.
    Alternatively, students can be asked to write a report on the book and class discussions can center on those reports. The best reports can also be read to the class.

2. For the day this article is due: Students can write an introspec-tive essay on their own ethnic identification, making comparisons, where appropriate, with Rodriguez's analysis.

3. In small groups: How can Rodriguez maintain a Chicano identity if he were to complete his Ph.D. and to teach at an American college or university? Is this a worthwhile goal? Or should he give it up, much as did Americans of German and British ancestry during the preceding generations?

4. In small groups: Discuss how "roots" are related to people's sense of identity and their well-being. What kinds of roots? Why is ethnic identity (or "roots") more important for some groups than for others?

Introduction to Part I: "The Sociological Perspective"

I. Multiple-Choice

1. The potential of sociology is that it can provide:
    a. comfortable ways of looking at things
    b. old light to shine on new things   c. complacent assumptions
    <u>d</u>. a look behind the scenes   e. none of the above

2. The quality of mind that allows us to see beyond our immediate
    confines in order to understand the broader social and historical
    forces at work in our lives is called:
    <u>a</u>. the sociological imagination   b. confinement removal
    c. recollective transience   d. mental analysis
    e. social analysis

II. True-False

T 1. Sociology is an academic discipline centering on understanding
       the general context in which people live and analyzing how
       their lives are influenced by that context.

Article 1. Berger, "Invitation to Sociology"

I. Multiple-Choice

1. The sociologist is a person primarily interested in the doings of:
    a. animals   b. plants   c. electrons   <u>d</u>. people   e. insects

2. Sociologists are motivated primarily by their:
    a. voyeurism   <u>b</u>. curiosity   c. sadism   d. masochism
    e. challenges

3. With which of the following are sociologists the <u>least</u> interested?
    a. actions   b. relationships   c. institutions   d. ideas
    <u>e</u>. climate

4. On the sociological journey to knowledge, the traveler whose path
    the sociologist is most likely to cross is the:
    a. biologist   b. psychologist   <u>c</u>. historian
    d. political scientist   e. economist

5. The sociologist is <u>least</u> likely to study:
    a. power   b. status   c. class   <u>d</u>. motivation   e. ethnicity

6. It can be said that the first wisdom of sociology is:
    a. Things are usually what they seem
    b. Don't waste time questioning the obvious
    c. Most people are interested in power
    <u>d</u>. Things often are not what they seem
    e. Money is the major motivator of human behavior

46

7. The impact of a totally new culture on someone is known as:
   a. electro shock   b. culture shock   c. a rude awakening
   d. the eye-opening experience   e. future shock

8. Like the anthropologist, the sociologist experiences reactions of
   excitement and awe at the things he or she discovers. Unlike most
   anthropologists, however, sociologists do not have to:
   a. leave their own society or culture   b. obtain research grants
   c. observe human behavior   d. record their observations
   e. consult anyone else

9. Pick the phrase that best refers to the sudden illumination of new
   and unexpected facets of human existence in society:
   a. the humanistic justification of sociology   b. culture shock
   c. the essence of anthropology   d. the downfall of sociology
   e. the cross between sociology and history

10. Which word or phrase best describes what sociology is to someone
    engaged in sociological discovery?
    a. a pastime   b. a job   c. a passion   d. a delight
    e. a routine

11. Berger says that the primary motivation of sociologists is:
    a. curiosity   b. wealth   c. security
    d. academic advancement   e. fame

II. True-False

F 1. Although sociologists study almost every aspect of life in
      society, they stay away from things that are too profane or too
      sacred.
T 2. Motivated by an intense desire to know what is "really
      happening," what is going on "behind the scenes," sociologists
      study almost every aspect of life in society.
F 3. When one penetrates beneath the surface and peers behind the
      masks that individuals and organizations wear, one sees the
      reality that is put forward for public consumption.
F 4. In their quest for understanding, sociologists move through the
      world with respect for people's usual lines of demarcation.
T 5. The questions that sociologists ask lead them to all levels of
      society.
T 6. The sociological quest for understanding sometimes takes
      sociologists into matters that others regard as too sacred or
      too distasteful for dispassionate investigation.
T 7. The main question sociologists ask concerns the ultimate signi-
      ficance of what people do.
T 8. For the sociologist, his or her own life inevitably becomes a
      part of the subject matter being studied.
T 9. There is a deceptive simplicity and obviousness about some
      sociological investigations.
F 10. Social reality has a single layer of meaning. It is the
      penetration of this layer that is the goal of sociology.

III. Essay

47

1. Of what value is sociology?
2. What does Berger mean by the phrase "the excitement of sociology"?
3. Briefly describe how Berger used the example of race and caste to illustrate how sociology can add a new perspective to an old issue, how sociology can shed "new light" on something with which we are already familiar.
4. Briefly describe the type of person who would <u>not</u> be interested in the study of sociology. Based on Berger's analysis, what type of person would be interested in studying sociology?
5. How does curiosity play a role in sociological studies?
6. Why might sociology be termed a "dangerous" study?

Article 2. Henslin, "Sociology and the Social Sciences"

I. Multiple-Choice

1. The explanations of the social world that the ancients developed were largely based on:
   a. rationalistic interpretations   b. revelation
   c. systematic observations   <u>d</u>. magic and superstitition
   e. elucidations

2. Which of the following is sometimes excluded from the listing of social sciences?
   <u>a</u>. history   b. sociology   c. political science   d. economics
   e. anthropology

3. Identify the term that refers to factors or characteristics that sociologists measure in order to understand human behavior better.
   a. causers   b. causations   <u>c</u>. variables   d. variators
   e. formators

4. The social science most interested in how people attain the ruling position in their society is:
   <u>a</u>. political science   b. sociology   c. anthropology
   d. psychology   e. history

5. The social science that concentrates on the production, distribution, and allocation of the material goods and services of a society is:
   a. political science   <u>b</u>. economics   c. anthropology
   d. sociology   e. history

6. The culture of preliterate peoples would most likely be the focus of the:
   a. political scientist   b. economist   <u>c</u>. anthropologist
   d. sociologist   e. historian

7. The science that concentrates its efforts on processes that occur within the individual is:
   a. anthropology   b. sociology   <u>c</u>. psychology   d. history
   e. economics

8. The social science that does <u>not</u> focus on the study of human behavior is:
   a. economics   b. history   c. psychology

48

d. political science   e. none of the above

9. In studying juvenile delinquency, the social scientist who is the
    most likely to focus on the levels or dimensions of power within a
    gang of delinquents is the:
    a. political scientist   b. economist   c. anthropologist
    d. psychologist   e. historian

10. What juvenile delinquency costs the nation would most likely be
    the focus of the:
    a. political scientist   b. economist   c. anthropologist
    d. sociologist   e. historian

11. The implements that delinquents use to commit crimes, as well as
    the belief system of delinquents, would most likely be the focus
    of the:
    a. sociologist   b. economist   c. psychologist
    d. anthropologist   e. psychologist

12. The social scientist most likely to be interested in cross-
    cultural comparisons of juvenile delinquency would be the:
    a. political scientist   b. economist   c. historian
    d. anthropologist   e. psychologist

13. The social science that has the broadest, or most encompassing,
    approach to the study of human behavior is:
    a. sociology   b. economics   c. political science
    d. anthropology   e. psychology

14. The social scientist most likely to stress social class as a
    variable in juvenile gang membership is the:
    a. economist   b. political scientist   c. sociologist
    d. historian   e. psychologist

15. In studying juvenile delinquency, which social scientist is the
    most likely to emphasize police discretion, the judicial process,
    and norms?
    a. the economist   b. the political scientist
    c. the sociologist   d. the historian   e. the psychologist

16. The overarching social science is:
    a. economics   b. political science   c. sociology   d. history
    e. psychology

17. The two major forms of sociology are:
    a. processual and functional   b. major and minor
    c. relativistic and absolutistic
    d. institutional and interactional   e. the old and the new

18. The term that refers to a group's special language is:
    a. torga   b. argot   c. margot   d. torgam
    e. speech of transference

19. The term sociologists use to refer to what people do in one
    another's presence is:
    a. coordinates   b. relationships   c. actions and reactions

<u>d</u>. face-to-face interaction   e. presence of mind

20. The term that sociologists use to refer to the behaviors that
    people expect of others is:
    a. retroactions   b. expectations   <u>c</u>. norms   d. interactions
    e. fulminations

21. Sociologists refer to recurring aspects of human behavior as:
    <u>a</u>. patterned relationships   b. interactions
    c. actions and reactions   d. recurring behavior
    e. transferences

II. True-False

F 1. Although people in ancient times developed explanations for the
      natural world, they did not develop explanations for the social
      world.
F 2. The natural sciences are divided and subdivided into special-
      ized fields, or areas of research. The social sciences are
      not.
T 3. Both the natural and social worlds contain ordered relation-
      ships that are not obvious but must be abstracted by means of
      controlled and repeated observations.
T 4. History is sometimes excluded from the listing of social
      sciences.
F 5. Anthropology is the social science that concentrates primarily
      on the production, distribution, and allocation of goods and
      services of a society.
T 6. Psychology is the social science that concentrates its efforts
      on studying processes that occur within the individual.
F 7. The social sciences differ from one another primarily in the
      content of what they study, rather than in their approaches or
      orientations to what they study.
T 8. All the social sciences study human behavior.
F 9. In studying a juvenile delinquent gang, the primary focus of
      the psychologist would likely be the levels or dimensions of
      power within the gang.
F 10. Of all the social sciences, the historian has the broadest
      approach to the study of human behavior.
T 11. Argot is a term that refers to a group's special language.
T 12. Sociologists use the term face-to-face interaction to refer to
      what people do in one another's presence.
T 13. The term norms refers to the behaviors that people expect of
      others.
T 14. Institutional and interactional are the two major forms of
      sociology.

III. Essay

1. Compare and contrast the social sciences: history, political
   science, economics, anthropology, psychology, and sociology.
2. Explain why it is accurate to say that sociology is the broadest
   of the social sciences.
3. If historians, political scientists, economists, anthropologists,
   psychologists, and sociologists were to study juvenile
   delinquency, how are they likely to differ in their research?

4. If historians, political scientists, economists, anthropologists, psychologists, and sociologists were to study one country's armed invasion of another, how are they likely to differ?

Article 3. Mills, "The Promise"

I. Multiple-Choice

1. Seeing how the unique historical circumstances of a society affect people, and at the same time seeing how people affect history is called:
    a. the historical perspective   b. the economic outlook
    c. the marvels of the imagination   d. biography and history
    e. the sociological imagination

2. The sociological imagination is also known as:
    a. the historical perspective   b. the sociological perspective
    c. the economic outlook   d. the political science factor
    e. the master component

3. Which of the following is not a capacity of the sociological imagination?
    a. to shift from the political to the psychological
    b. to shift from the examination of a single family to the comparative assessment of the national budgets of the world
    c. to shift from the theological school to the military establishment
    d. to shift from the considerations of an oil industry to the studies of contemporary poetry
    e. all the above are part of the capacity of the sociological imagination

4. The sociological imagination can be said to be a form of:
    a. other-directedness   b. inner-directedness
    c. Chaucerian reasoning   d. self-consciousness
    e. none of the above

5. Private matters, in the sense that they occur within the character of the individual and within the range of his or her immediate relations with others, are defined by Mills as:
    a. factors   b. troubles   c. issues
    d. the perplexity of modern society   e. none of the above

6. According to Mills, the following term refers to matters which transcend local environments of the individual and the range of one's inner life:
    a. issues   b. problems   c. troubles   d. values
    e. none of the above

7. When people cherish some set of values and do not feel any threat to them, they experience:
    a. lethargy   b. well-being   c. catharsis   d. empathy
    e. indifference

8. If people are neither aware of any cherished values nor experience any threat to them, they experience:

a. anger   b. rage   c. indifference   d. contentment
e. anxiety

9. If people are unaware of any cherished values but are still very
    much aware of a threat, they experience:
    a. apathy   b. uneasiness   c. anger   d. empathy
    e. sympathy

10. Which of the following does Mills identify as the signal feature
    of our time?
    a. indifference and uneasiness   b. anger and rage
    c. oppression and depression   d. guilt and remorse
    e. empathy and sympathy

II. True-False

T 1. Every individual lives out his or her life in a particular
       society, and the historical circumstances of that society
       greatly influence what that individual becomes.
T 2. People are not only shaped by their society but they also
       contribute to the shaping of their own society and to the
       course of its history.
T 3. The facts of contemporary history are also facts about the
       success and failure of individual men and women.
T 4. Neither the life of an individual nor the history of a society
       can be understood without understanding both.
T 5. World history now affects everyone.
T 6. In what Mills calls the overdeveloped world, the means of
       authority and violence are becoming total in scope and
       bureaucratic in form.
T 7. The very shaping of history now outpaces the ability of people
       to orient themselves in accordance with cherished values.
T 8. The sociological imagination enables one to understand one's
       experiences and gauge one's fate by locating oneself within
       one's historical period.
F 9. A major drawback of the sociological imagination is that it
       does not allow us to grasp history and biography and the
       relationship between the two.
F 10. According to Mills, "people's chief enemy and danger is their
       own unruly nature and the dark forces pent up within them."
T 11. Mills says that in our present troubled historical
       circumstances, our most needed quality of mind is the
       sociological imagination.

III. Essay

1. Describe what Mills means by the term, "the sociological imagina-
    tion."
2. Of what value is the sociological imagination?
3. Mills says that nowadays people have a feeling of being trapped by
    the private orbits in which they live. According to Mills, what
    underlies this feeling? How might the sociological imagination
    help?
4. Classic sociologists who have been imaginatively aware of the
    promise of their work have consistently asked three sorts of
    questions, says Mills. What are those questions?

5. Mills says that the sociological imagination has become our most
    needed quality of mind today. Why is it needed so badly?

Introduction to Part II: "Doing Sociological Research"

I. Multiple-Choice

1. The two major activities of science are:
    a. experiments and interviews   b. teaching and experiments
    c. experimental conclusions and empirical research
    d. theory and research

2. The term for how sociologists do their research is:
    a. sociological theory   b. empirical observations
    c. research methods   d. empirical conclusions

3. An explanation for how pertinent facts fit together is the
    definition of:
    a. theory   b. research   c. empiricism
    d. symbolic interaction

4. The theory that has these major points: (1) human beings have a
    self, (2) people construct meaning and act on the basis of that
    meaning, and (3) people take into account the possible reactions
    of others:
    a. symbolic interaction   b. functionalism   c. conflict theory
    d. empirical theory

5. The theory that stresses that society is an integrated system made
    up of various parts:
    a. symbolic interaction   b. functionalism   c. conflict theory
    d. empirical theory

6. The theory that views society as a system in which the various
    parts compete for a larger share of resources--and there is not
    enough to go around to satisfy each group:
    a. symbolic interaction   b. functionalism   c. conflict theory
    d. empirical theory

II. True-False

T 1. Empirical means based on objective observations.

Article 4: Henslin, "How Sociologists Do Research"

I. Multiple-Choice

1. To illustrate research methods, the author focuses on how sociolo-
    gists gather information on:
    a. rapists and their victims   b. prostitution   c. the homeless
    d. pornographers

2. The topics that sociologists study are determined by:
    a. government officials who provide guidelines

b. a priority list drawn up by the college or university
c. fellow faculty members
d. the sociologist's own curiosity and interests

3. Research methods are:
a. a statement of what you expect to find according to predictions from a theory
b. factors expressed in a relationship that are thought to be significant
c. ways sociologists collect data
d. also called sociological theory

4. The term secondary analysis refers to:
a. psychotherapy   b. a research method
c. birth order analysis
d. research being replicated by another researcher

5. Having people answer a series of questions is the definition of:
a. a survey   b. documents   c. secondary analysis
d. unobtrusive measures

6. If you want to generalize to a population, this is the kind of sample you want:
a. unobtrusive sample   b. collective sample   c. random sample
d. complementary sample

7. Surveys in which respondents are asked questions directly, usually face-to-face, are:
a. not respected in the scientific community
b. called interviews   c. called questionnaires
d. no longer used

8. If you use personal diaries and books, videotapes and movies, or police reports and bank records to research social life, you are using this method:
a. experiment   b. survey   c. independent variable
d. documents

9. This research method is seldom used by sociologists:
a. questionnaires   b. interviews   c. experiments
d. unobtrusive measures

10. Independent variables are defined as:
a. factors that cause a change in something
b. factors that stand independent from the scrutiny of researchers
c. interviewees who assert their independence by refusing to answer questions
d. factors that are changed

II. True-False

F   1. Sociological research shows that men rape because they are sexually deprived.
F   2. What a woman wears is a major factor in determining whether or not she will become a victim of rape.

F 3. The author presents a model of social research, including a diagram that illustrates the various steps. There are three steps in this research model.
F 4. It is important to define a sociological problem in the broadest possible terms. The more general the research question, the more likely the researcher is to uncover more information.
T 5. A hypothesis is a statement of what you expect to find according to predictions from a theory.
T 6. The term "variable" refers to factors that are thought to be significant.
F 7. The method a sociologist uses to collect data is called a hypothesis.
T 8. Validity means the extent to which an operational definition measures what you intend to measure.
T 9. Reliability refers to the extent to which your measure and studies give consistent results.
F 10. All sociological research has at least one hypothesis.

III. Essay

1. Explain what a random sample is. What are its advantages and disadvantages?
2. Explain the use of interviews in conducting surveys. What are their advantages? Disadvantages? Give examples.
3. What is secondary analysis? What are some of the problems associated with it? What are its advantages?
4. Explain the difference between common sense and sociology.
5. Explain the research process. You may refer to the eight-step model presented in the article.

Article 5: Scully and Marolla, "Riding the Bull at Gilley's"

I. Multiple-Choice

1. What was the main question that Scully and Marolla set out to answer?
   a. Does prison rehabilitate rapists?
   b. Do rapists feel remorse or guilt?
   c. Why do men rape?   d. When do most rapes occur?

2. The authors interviewed:
   a. men who had been sent to prison for rape
   b. female victims of rape
   c. males who had been raped in prison
   d. law enforcement officials who had been assigned to rape cases

3. The view that rapists lack the ability to control their behavior, that rapists are "sick" individuals from the "lunatic fringe" of society, is held by:
   a. psychopathologists   b. symbolic interactionists
   c. transcendentalists   d. sociomolecularists

4. A central assumption in the psychopathological model is that male sexual aggression is:
   a. normal   b. learned   c. healthy   d. unusual or strange

5. From the feminist perspective, rape is seen as:
   a. reversionary animalistic gratification
   b. an act of uncontrollable passion
   c. an act of violence and social control   d. mental illness

6. A content analysis of 428 "adult only" books showed that:
   a. men were portrayed as victims about 40 percent of the time
   b. rape was presented as part of normal male/female relations
   c. men who raped were portrayed as ashamed but gratified
   d. rape was not a prevalent theme

7. Some rapists account for their actions by asserting a "collective liability." This means that:
   a. any person is liable to be a victim if they owe money and someone goes to collect it
   b. each rapist is accountable for his own actions
   c. the rapist justifies his actions because he thinks the victim enjoyed it
   d. punishment was directed at the victim because she represented a woman whom the offenders perceived as collectively responsible for their problems

8. In an effort to change public attitudes that are damaging to the victims of rape, many writers emphasize:
   a. the psychopathological character of the offender
   b. how women unknowingly invite unwanted sexual advances
   c. the passionate aspect of sexual offenses
   d. the violent, brutal, and aggressive character of rape

9. For the past 20 years, national data based on reported rapes and victimization studies indicate that the rate of:
   a. black on white rape significantly exceeds the rate of white on black rape
   b. white on black rape significantly exceeds the rate of black on white rape
   c. Hispanic on white rape significantly exceeds the rate of white on Hispanic rape
   d. white on Hispanic rape significantly exceeds the rate of Hispanic on white rape

10. Malmuth and his fellow researchers concluded that in the final analysis the objective of most rapists is:
   a. sexual gratification   b. dominance
   c. excitement from the risk of being apprehended   d. robbery

II. True-False

F 1. Empirical research has uncovered a personality type or character disorder that reliably discriminates rapists from other groups of men.

F 2. Research shows that nearly 95 percent of rapists were psychotic when they raped.

T 3. The psychopathological model ignores evidence that links sexual aggression to environmental variables which suggest that rape is a learned behavior.

T   4.   Data from preindustrial societies show the existence of rape-
         free cultures.
T   5.   The authors say that the United States is among the most rape-
         prone of all societies.
F   6.   The psychopathologists take the position that rape is a
         deliberate criminal act, rather than subconscious and
         uncontrollable.
T   7.   Among the Cheyenne, rape was an acceptable way to punish a wife
         who was thought to be unfaithful.
F   8.   The sample used by Scully and Marolla was random. Therefore,
         we know how to precisely generalize these findings to the
         larger population.
T   9.   Many of the men in this sample had been convicted of a burglary
         or robbery in connection with rape.
T 10.   Most rapes in the United States are intraracial.

III. Essay

1.   How does the sociological analysis of rape differ from the psycho-
     pathological view? Discuss the implications of each view.
2.   What is the feminist view of rape? How do feminists view
     pornography?
3.   Why do men rape?
4.   Assume that you are the governor of your state and that you have
     just been awarded a $25 million grant to reduce rape. Based on
     the information contained in this article, what steps should you
     take?

Article 6: Chagnon, "Doing Fieldwork Among the Yanomamo"

I. Multiple-Choice

1.   The Yanomamo are best described as what kind of people?
     a. gentle   b. fierce   c. cowardly   d. diplomatic

2.   Napoleon Chagnon is a(n):
     a. economist   b. sociologist   c. anthropologist
     d. archeologist

3.   This aspect of Yanomamo life sets them apart from most other
     tribal societies:
     a. electricity and running water   b. warfare
     c. cannibalism   d. matriarchy

4.   One of the first things Chagnon observed when he arrived to study
     the Yanomamo was:
     a. how tidy and neat everything was
     b. the television antennas on the huts
     c. the length of the braids on the male tribal leaders
     d. men blowing hallucinogenic drugs up their noses

5.   James P. Barker, who introduced Chagnon to the Yanomamo, was a(n):
     a. British engineer assigned to South America to build a dam and a
        generating plant
     b. American Naval Officer   c. missionary   d. anthropologist

6. Chagnon uses this term to refer to the lies he told the Yanomamo about his food:
   <u>a</u>. adaptive defense mechanisms   b. experimental research devices
   c. cultural transmission vehicles   d. necessary evils

7. This is the Yanomamo's most common form of greeting:
   a. "Health to you and yours"   b. a ceremonial bow
   c. "Friend or foe?"   <u>d</u>. "I am hungry"

8. Shortly after he arrived in the field, several Yanomamo men became friendly with Chagnon. Their friendship was a pretext to:
   a. get his money   <u>b</u>. loot his possessions
   c. raise their own status in the tribe through their association with him
   d. marry their daughters to him

9. In order to get along with the Yanomamo, the author:
   <u>a</u>. became sly, aggressive, and intimidating
   b. gave away all his possessions
   c. gave canoe rides to the females and hunted for the men
   d. reluctantly participated in raids on other tribes

10. What time-consuming, difficult task did Chagnon undertake?
    a. building a bridge   b. teaching English
    <u>c</u>. recording genealogies   d. cultivating a garden

II. True-False

T 1. The Yanomamo Indians live in southern Venezuela and northern Brazil.
F 2. The author, who has studied the Yanomamo as well as other tribal groups, states that aggression is an important part of the culture of primitive people everywhere.
F 3. Before he set out on his fieldwork, Chagnon did extensive library research on the Yanomamo to familiarize himself with their language and customs.
T 4. The Yanomamo were not interested in eating Chagnon's peanut butter because it looked like animal feces to them.
T 5. Food sharing is important to the Yanomamo as a means of displaying friendship.
T 6. The Yanomamo considered Chagnon to be subhuman because he was a non-Yanomamo.
F 7. Although there were times when the Yanomamo needed something that Chagnon possessed, such as food or tools, they were too proud to ask him for it.
T 8. Beating one's wife with a club is an accepted way of demonstrating ferocity among the Yanomamo.
T 9. The Yanomamo do not use a person's name after the person dies.

III. Essay

1. Explain how the Yanomamo differed from the preconceived ideas that Chagnon had about what it would be like to live among primitive people.
2. What obstacles did Chagnon encounter in recording genealogies, and how did he overcome them?

3. What defense mechanisms did Chagnon develop in order to get along with the Yanomamo?
4. Why are the Yanomamo so violent?
5. Contrast the masculine and feminine roles in Yanomamo society.

Introduction to Part III: "The Cultural Context of Social Life"

I. Multiple-Choice

1. That which people most take for granted is:
   a. their own culture   b. the weather   c. education
   d. the city water supply   e. the future

2. The term for clothing, speech, mannerisms, beliefs, values, and so on, is:
   a. communication   b. ideas   c. rituals   d. behavior
   e. culture

3. The area of the world in which people do not assume "first come, first served" but, rather, assume that people will push and crowd one another in order to get served is:
   a. Outer Mongolia   b. Scandinavia   c. Northern Africa
   d. Southeast Asia   e. South America

II. True-False

F 1. As used by sociologists, the term culture refers to things external to people, to things that do not affect one's thinking.
T 2. The practice of "first come, first served" is an example of culture.
T 3. The term culture shock refers to the situation of someone being in a culture so strange that the person can no longer depend on the basics of social interactions which that person has learned from childhood.

III. Essay

1. Define culture, and briefly describe its effects on people.

Article 7: Miner, "Body Ritual Among the Nacirema"

I. Multiple-Choice

1. The magical beliefs and practices of the Nacirema present a good example of:
   a. premarital sexual behavior   b. an undeveloped civilization
   c. voodoo   d. female infanticide
   e. the extremes to which human behavior can go

2. The Nacirema reside in:
   a. Asia   b. North America   c. South America   d. Europe
   e. Africa

59

3. Miner found that the appearance and health of their _____
   loomed largest as a dominant concern in the ethos of the Nacirema:
   a. housing   b. clothing   c. land   d. automobiles
   e. bodies

4. The opulence of a Nacirema house is often judged by the number it
   possesses of which of the following?
   a. dogs   b. closets   c. cats   d. wives   e. shrines

5. Part of the process the Nacirema use to cure their various
   illnesses involves writing in an ancient and secret language. Who
   does the writing?
   a. medicine men   b. the mothers
   c. the tribal chief   d. the fathers
   e. the individual who is ailing; if he or she is too ill to write,
      the task is taken over by scribes for this purpose

6. Because the Nacirema have so many real and imagined maladies, each
   household contains a:
   a. scribe for writing in an ancient and secret language
   b. charm-box   c. shrine in memory of the departed
   d. holy-mouth specialist (but only in the homes of the wealthy)
   e. wall on which crutches and other memorabilia of past illnesses
      are hung in order to remind the household members of the
      frailty of human health

7. As part of their ceremony, what do Nacirema women bake in a small
   oven for about an hour?
   a. potatoes   b. bread   c. their heads
   d. fresh meat killed by the hunter of the family   e. pottery

8. Every community of any size has an imposing temple dedicated to
   making sick people healthy. Here elaborate ceremonies are
   performed. One such ceremony involves:
   a. stripping the supplicant of his or her clothes
   b. an examination by holy-mouth men
   c. divulging the contents of the home shrine-box
   d. a death enactment, "just in case"   e. none of the above

9. Those who stay in the temple dedicated to making the sick people
   healthy (even though temporarily) lose their body secrecy. Their
   bathing and excretory acts while in the temple are often performed
   naked and in the presence of:
   a. mother   b. father   c. brothers   d. sisters
   e. vestal maidens

10. The following type of "witch doctors" or "medicine men" has the
    power to exorcise the devils lodged in the heads of people who
    have been bewitched:
    a. speakers   b. listeners   c. mutes   d. scribes
    e. the masked

II. True-False

T 1. The fundamental belief underlying the cultural patterns of the
       Nacirema appears to be that the human body is ugly in its

natural state and that its natural tendency is to debility and disease.

T 2. The Nacirema believe that the way of overcoming the natural tendency of the human body is through ritual and ceremony.
T 3. Every Nacirema household has one or more shrines devoted to the care of the body.
F 4. To be certain they are carried out correctly, the rituals associated with Nacirema body care are done with most family members present.
T 5. The Nacirema appear to believe that a strong relationship exists between oral and moral characteristics.
T 6. The daily rituals performed by the Nacirema include a mouth-rite.
F 7. The _latipso_ is the village idiot.
T 8. As part of their body-rites, many Nacirema women bake their heads in small ovens.
T 9. Because the Nacirema believe that parents bewitch their own children, especially while teaching them secret body rituals, they seek witch doctors who use counter-magic.
T 10. General dissatisfaction with breast shape among Nacirema women is due to the fact that the idea form is virtually outside the range of human variation.
T 11. Among the Nacirema studied by Linton, sexual intercourse appeared to be taboo as a topic and scheduled as an act.
F 12. Because their body rituals have held them back, the Nacirema have been unable to develop an advanced civilization.

III. Essay

1. Why should the Nacirema be studied? Of what value is understanding their way of life?
2. Describe the function of the "holy-mouth-men."
3. Describe briefly the process employed to exorcise one who is bewitched.
4. Discuss the practices of the Nacirema (at the time the article was written) concerning pregnancy, childbirth, and birth control.
5. Discuss the role of magic in the lives of the Nacirema.

Article 8: Caplow, "The American Way of Celebrating Christmas"

I. Multiple-Choice

1. According to the tree rule in Middletown, who should not put up Christmas trees?
    a. married couples without children
    b. married couples with children
    c. unmarried persons with no living children
    d. widowed, divorced, or adoptive parents

2. Middletowners find that the ideal time to photograph recipients of Christmas gifts is when they are:
    a. putting the present away   b. saying "thank you" to the giver
    c. opening the gift at the moment of "surprise"
    d. using the gift for the very first time

3. Rooms in which Christmas gifts are given have the distinction of:

a. not being used for any other purpose on the day that gifts are exchanged
b. also being the room in which the annual family feast is held
c. being decorated with Christmas emblems
d. not being cleaned until the day after Christmas

4. According to the scaling rules, which gift should have the greatest value?
a. one from a child to either parent
b. one from a parent to a child
c. one from a husband to a wife
d. one from a sibling to a sibling

5. A Middletown resident who is confined by severe illness:
a. receives gifts, but is excused from giving them
b. is excused from the gift exchange ritual because Middletowners feel that to receive gifts without giving them would be too embarrassing
c. delegates others to do his or her shopping and wrapping
d. gives cash instead of shopping for gifts

6. Middletown children were offended by gifts that were:
a. better suited to members of the opposite sex
b. educational   c. too "young"   d. cheap

7. Middletowners are concerned that gifts exchanged between _____ be of approximately equal value:
a. husbands and wives   b. parents and children   c. siblings
d. grandparents and grandchildren

8. Caplow says that Christmas gift-giving is a language for expressing:
a. social status   b. power   c. how much one values another
d. gratitude for being alive another Christmas season

9. Caplow found that failing to give a gift may signify:
a. severe economic hardship
b. that the parties involved are so intimate that the absence of a gift between them does not matter
c. the desire to terminate a relationship
d. the onset of senility

II. True-False

T 1. Christmas trees in Middletown are not set up in undecorated rooms.
T 2. During the 24-hour period following Christmas Eve, the average Middletowner attends more than three gatherings at which a feast and gifts are exchanged.
F 3. Middletowner husbands and fathers who are off work for the holiday help prepare traditional Christmas dinners.
T 4. Middletowners believe that the economic value of a giver's gift should be scaled to the emotional value of the relationship.
T 5. According to Caplow's scaling of gifts in Middletown, siblings should be valued equally in childhood but not later.
F 6. In Middletown, money is considered an appropriate gift from

senior to junior kin, as well as from junior to senior kin.

F 7. The reciprocity rule requires that the gifts people exchange be
       of equal value.
T 8. Middletown husbands often give more valuable gifts to their
       wives than they receive from them.
F 9. Caplow found that the rules of Christmas gift-giving in
       Middletown are so explicit that they are even included in books
       of etiquette.
F 10. Caplow found that five forms of moral disapproval are leveled
       at offenders who violate the rules of Christmas gift-giving,
       including ostracism from future gatherings.

III. Essay

1. Describe the Christmas gift-giving ritual in Middletown.
2. Briefly explain the scaling rules for gift-giving.
3. How is gift-giving like a language? What does gift-giving
    communicate?

Article 9: Goffman, "The Presentation of Self in Everyday Life"

I. Multiple-Choice

1. Precautions taken to avoid discrepancies in the image an individ-
    ual is endeavoring to project are called:
    a. discrepancy avoidance devices   b. defensive practices
    c. justification mechanisms   d. modes of preservation
    e. manipulative strategies

2. "Expressions given" refer to:
    a. behavior thought to be under the control of the actor
    b. behavior thought to be not under the control of the actor
    c. the directions given to actors by stage directors
    d. behavior thought to be due to inherited characteristics
    e. appeals for help

3. A working consensus is:
    a. the basic agreements within which face-to-face interaction
       takes place
    b. a mutual show of affection, respect, and concern
    c. a compromise to satisfy the merging interests of two factions
    d. more common among whites than among blacks
    e. stronger than an initial consensus

4. When an individual enters the presence of others, those others
    commonly seek information about the individual. This can best be
    explained as:
    a. a self-centered move on the part of the others
    b. an expression of genuine concern on the part of the others
    c. hospitality   d. the Goffman theorem   e. none of the above

5. Goffman presents a _____ model of human life:
    a. pluralistic   b. monolithic   d. dialectic
    d. dramaturgical   e. futuristic

6. Protective and defensive practices constitute the techniques

employed to establish and maintain the impressions fostered while
a person is:
a. being socialized   b. in private situations
<u>c</u>. in the presence of others   d. challenging a projected image
e. planning future encounters

7. At this time individuals can more easily demand for themselves and
    extend to others some desired line of treatment:
    <u>a</u>. at the beginning of an encounter
    b. after rapport has been established
    c. after one has proven one's sincerity
    d. equally well throughout an encounter
    e. during an encounter's midpoint

8. The "parts" referred to in this article consist of:
    a. the lines one learns for repetitive interaction
    b. speaking parts only   c. customing   <u>d</u>. aspects of the front
    e. memory work

9. According to the dramaturgical model of human behavior, we:
    <u>a</u>. are better actors than we think   b. think, therefore we are
    c. stop acting after we arrive home
    d. play one major part in a lifetime   e. none of the above

10. The main difference between the dramaturgical model and the
    theater is:
    a. in everyday life, we have no stage
    b. productions are more successful in the theater
    <u>c</u>. in everyday life, we believe our roles
    d. costumes are worn in the theater   e. all of the above

11. The main goal of an actor during an interaction is to:
    a. be consistent with a particular audience
    b. be consistent in one's actions, clothing, manner, and
       expressions
    <u>c</u>. control audience response, especially those directed toward the
       actor
    d. elicit approval from others
    e. alter the other's definition of herself or himself

12. Information games have a cycle. That cycle includes:
    a. concealment   b. discovery   c. false revelation
    <u>d</u>. all of the above   e. none of the above

13. An agreement exists between the actor and audience in terms of:
    <u>a</u>. avoiding open conflict
    b. discovering the truth in a gaming matter
    c. avoiding the truth at all possible costs
    d. revealing each other's cover   e. avoiding transferences

14. The term "expressions given off" refers to:
    a. behavior thought to be under the control of the actor
    <u>b</u>. behavior thought to be not under the control of the actor
    c. olfactory sensory perceptions (such as from perfume)
    d. behaviors thought to be due to inherited characteristics
    e. challenges to the self-concept of the other

15. In order to project a particular "self" we:
    a. lie about ourselves   b. relax and just "be ourselves"
    c. manipulate various aspects of our biography and situation
    d. challenge the self of the other   e. all of the above

16. Sign activities are composed of:
    a. impressions   b. expressions   c. union members on strike
    d. postures   e. a and b above

17. Goffman refers to "defensive practices" used to save someone
    else's definition of a situation as:
    a. "saving and definition of the situation"   b. "social graces"
    c. "altruistic devices"   d. "protective practices"
    e. "manipulative strategies"

18. According to Goffman, which of the following statements is true?
    a. All humans are actors   b. All mothers love their children
    c. Honest people do not put on a show for others
    d. Dramaturgy refers to a medical treatment for bruises
    e. Situations demand rooted self-concepts

19. According to Goffman, which of the following statements is false?
    a. We are all like actors on the stage
    b. During interaction we use both protective and defensive
       practices
    c. We all act on what is called the definition of the situation
    d. The honest person is not an actor
    e. All of the above are true

II. True-False

T 1. Goffman presents a dramaturgical model of human life.
F 2. It has been said that we, as interacting human beings, spend
       out entire life play-acting--the stage is already set and our
       part(s) written. Therefore, we have no way of controlling the
       reaction of the audience.
F 3. In developing his dramaturgical idea, Goffman is saying that
       few people are sincere in their interaction with others.
F 4. An individual may be able to create a false impression with the
       words he/she chooses, but his/her true self is always revealed
       through modes of expression such as gestures and mannerisms.
F 5. Social perception entails a consideration of others and is
       therefore seldom self-centered.
F 6. According to Goffman, two kinds of communication are expres-
       sions given and expressions taken.
F 7. The expressiveness of an individual appears to involve two
       radically different kinds of sign activity: the expressions
       that one gives and the expressions that one takes.
T 8. When an individual is in the presence of others, his activity
       has a promissory character.
T 9. During interaction, participants tend to accept the defini-
       tional claims made by others who are present.
F 10. Although first impressions are important, it is not difficult
       to change the course of a relationship through the presentation
       of an altered self.

T 11. By acquiring information about an individual, we develop a definition of the situation.

F 12. In acquiring information about an individual, his/her social status is of little or no importance because America is not a class-conscious society.

T 13. From the dramaturgical model of human behavior that Goffman presents, one can logically conclude that human interaction is basically manipulative.

T 14. The major difference between everyday life and the theater itself is that ordinarily we believe the various roles to which we are assigned by our position in society.

III. Essay

1. Discuss the importance of information gained through first impressions and its significance for the future expressions (or interaction).

2. Explain Goffman's dramaturgical model of human life. Use a hypothetical situation to illustrate its significant aspects.

3. What are some of your motives for trying to control the impressions that others have of you? What are some of the most effective ways that you bring about those impressions?

4. Goffman mentions two kinds of communication--expressions given and expressions given off. Explain the difference between these two types. Use examples in your answer.

5. What does Goffman mean by the "information game"? Apply this concept to some interaction situation with which you are intimately familiar.

Introduction to Part IV: "Socialization and Gender"

I. Multiple Choice

1. Learning to be like others, becoming a full-fledged member of a group (a process essential to our survival), is known as:
   a. maturation   b. socialism   c. socialization
   d. affixation   e. sex role

2. Which of the following is part of the socialization process?
   a. learning rules   b. learning values   c. learning facts
   d. learning expectations about how we should present the self in different social settings
   e. all of the above

3. Which of the following is an agent of socialization?
   a. teachers   b. relatives   c. friends   d. neighbors
   e. all of the above

4. The term that refers to a person's tendency to behavior in a similar manner in different situations is:
   a. socialization   b. master trait   c. dominance   d. sex role
   e. personality

5. The term that refers to a characteristic or role, not limited to a

specific situation but cutting across many aspects of social life, one that imparts identity to an individual in many situations, is:
a. socialization   b. master trait   c. dominance   d. sex role
e. personality

6. An example of a master trait is:
    a. sex role   b. dominance   c. personality   d. socialization
    e. clothing

II. True-False

F 1. Socialization is the process of being friendly or outgoing.
T 2. Socialization refers to learning to become a full-fledged member of a group.
T 3. Socialization into sexuality is a major part of identity formation.
F 4. Personality is inborn, not the result of socialization.
T 5. Personality is not inborn, but is the result of socialization.

III. Essay

1. What is sex role socialization? Why is our sex role an example of a master trait?
2. What is socialization? What area of life does it involve?

Article 10: Davis, "Extreme Isolation"

I. Multiple-Choice

1. Anna was unwanted and badly neglected because she was:
    a. illegitimate   b. not a boy, as her parents expected
    c. the eighth child born to a very poor family
    d. deformed from birth defects resulting from either her mother's alcoholism or the unsafe medication her mother took
    e. none of the above

2. During her first 5-1/2 months, Anna lived in:
    a. a minister's home   b. two different children's homes
    c. the home of a man and woman who sought to adopt Anna
    d. all of the above   e. none of the above

3. For nearly the first six years of her life, Anna's diet consisted of only:
    a. fruits and vegetables   b. cow's milk   c. meat and water
    d. bread and water   e. oatmeal and other cereals

4. During the years she lived at her grandfather's house:
    a. Anna's mother gave her excellent care
    b. Anna's grandfather played with her and sang to her
    c. Anna's mother and grandmother left her alone day and night
    d. only the baby sitter gave Anna loving attention
    e. Anna's life was what most people would call ideal

5. After Anna was discovered, she was removed from the country home in which she had been living. She then was placed in a(n):
    a. apartment with her mother   b. foster home

c. children's home for possible adoption
d. private home for retarded children   e. mental hospital

6. Anna died from:
   a. complications from the beating she was given in her new home
   b. an automobile collision   c. overmedication
   d. unknown factors   e. hemorrhagic jaundice

7. By the time she died, Anna had attained the ability to:
   a. ride a bicycle   b. count to 100
   c. repeat words, build with blocks, and string beads
   d. speak like most children and dial a telephone
   e. all of the above

8. Isabelle's case was similar to Anna's in that both girls:
   a. had been isolated in a dark room for years
   b. appeared to be feeble-minded when they were discovered
   c. were illegitimate   d. all of the above   e. none of the above

9. Which answer best describes Isabelle's progress after she was
   found?
   a. a slow start followed by very rapid advancement through the
      usual stages of learning
   b. repeated failures
   c. a rapid advancement in the beginning, a tapering off, and then
      a rapid decline
   d. nothing short of amazing as she shortly surpassed most children
      of her age
   e. the inability to verbalize, but an amazing ability to pantomime
      and to dramatize situations

10. The speed with which Isabelle reached the normal level of mental
    development seems analogous to the way in which:
    a. chicks are hatched from eggs   b. seed is germinated
    c. a growing child recovers body weight following an illness
    d. echoes resound from a cavern   e. frogs jump

11. Isabelle's teachers reported that she was:
    a. inhibited, shy, and very self-conscious
    b. a "tattle-tale" who constantly sought sympathy from adults
    c. participating normally in all school activities
    d. a trouble-maker   e. displaying uncooperative attitudes

12. The author hypothesizes that if, like Isabelle, Anna had almost
    immediately received intensive speech therapy, Anna's development:
    a. probably would not have changed   b. might have slowed up
    c. would have surpassed Isabelle's
    d. might have been much more rapid than it was
    e. none of the above

13. The case of Isabelle demonstrates that:
    a. the acquisition of cultural skills after islation is almost
       impossible after an individual reaches the age of seven
    b. language development has little influence on the ability to
       understand culture
    c. children are born with primitive language

    d. it is possible to acquire language and cultural skills after
       years of extreme isolation
    e. none of the above

II. True-False

T 1. When Anna was removed from her grandfather's house when she was
     almost six years old, she could not talk, walk, or do anything
     that showed intelligence.

F 2. Anna made rapid progress after she was removed from her grand-
     father's house, and in just six months she was able to converse
     at the level of a five-year-old child.

T 3. Tests administered to Anna's mother when she was 32 revealed
     mental deficiency, and Anna was classified as a middle-grade
     moron.

T 4. When Anna and Isabelle were first discovered, people thought
     they were deaf.

T 5. It was initially thought that Isabelle was totally uneducable
     and that any attempt to teach her to speak would fail.

F 6. After her instruction began, it took Isabelle six years to
     learn what most children learn in two years.

T 7. Isabelle's mother was a deaf-mute.

F 8. After Isabelle was taught to speak and she was able to take the
     Stanford-Binet intelligence test, her score showed that she was
     in the near genius category.

F 9. After Anna was taught to speak, her score on the Stanford-Binet
     intelligence test showed that she had the native ability of the
     top ten percent of the population.

F 10. After they were discovered, Anna and Isabelle received approxi-
     mately the same prolonged, intensive, and expert training.

T 11. Isabelle's rapid development seems to have been due to her
     acquiring speech after she was discovered.

III. Essay

1. Compare the cases of Anna and Isabelle. In doing this, note the
   similarities and differences during both their years of isolation
   and the years following their discovery. To what do you attribute
   the differences in their development?
2. What does Davis mean by his concluding statement, "...only in
   these rare cases of extreme isolation is it possible 'to observe
   completely separated two factors in the development of human
   personality which are always otherwise only analytically
   separated, the biogenic and sociogenic factors'"?
3. From the evidence of Anna and Isabelle, what inference might we
   logically draw concerning human nature? In what ways do learning
   culture and acquiring a self-concept appear to depend on language?

Article 11: Henslin, "On Becoming Male"

I. Multiple-Choice

1. Which statement best represents the sociological perspective on
   masculinity and femininity?
   a. They are part of our genetic inheritance.
   b. They are part of our social inheritance.

c. There is no sociological perspective on this topic.
d. Masculinity and femininity are identical with gender.
e. There are more social influences on males than on females.

2. The method used to gather data for this article was:
    a. the author's experiences in "becoming" male
    b. the author's observations of the experience of others
    c. experiences students had shared with the author
    d. all of the above   e. none of the above

3. The clothing of children:
    a. expresses no sexuality
    b. is a means of grooming children for future adult roles
    c. is more significant for girls than it is for boys
    d. is utilitarian, not expressive   e. none of the above

4. To boys, the world of girls seems:
    a. foreign   b. desirable   c. fortunate   d. all of the above
    e. none of the above

5. According to this article, which of the following is likely to be
    the most prized aspect of the young male's experience?
    a. shopping trips with mommy
    b. attention and affection from daddy   c. freedom
    d. "masculine" toys   e. a sense of responsibility

6. According to the author, the world of boyhood can best be
    described as:
    a. restrictive, but fun   b. non-restrictive, but dull
    c. generally dull with occasional moments of high interest
    d. philosophically reflective
    e. full of freedom, fun, and challenge

7. According to this article, which of the following is among the
    worst punishments a boy can receive?
    a. being bound and gagged and thrown into a closet for three days
    b. being awakened every hour all night and day for a week
    c. being scolded   d. being grounded
    e. having his favorite toy taken away

8. According to this article, which of the following is the worst
    possible thing a boy can become?
    a. a sociologist   b. a "sissy"   c. a scholar   d. a teacher
    e. a failure at sports

9. Which of the following does the young American male learn upon
    entering the heterosexual world of adolescence and adulthood?
    a. to be an extremely adept role player
    b. to empathize with the female situation
    c. to strive for sexual equality
    d. to see his mother in a different light   e. none of the above

10. Which of the following terms does Henslin use to describe the sex
    role behaviors American males must display toward females upon
    reaching adolescence and adulthood?
    a. a farce   b. a game   c. a frantic race   d. a "hassle"

e. a blessing

11. The author says that the American socialization process ultimately forces males into _____, which greatly impedes the communication process with females and is a hindrance to good marital relationships.
   a. liking football   b. selfishness
   c. exaggerating their accomplishments and abilities
   d. subconscious hatred for females   e. artificiality

II. True-False

T 1. Men dominate the social institutions of the Western world.
F 2. Most sociologists agree that the basic reason that males dominate the social institutions is their genetic or biological heritage.
T 3. The author of this article agrees that while our gender is part of our biological inheritance, our sexuality (our masculinity or femininity) is part of our social inheritance.
T 4. Sociologists almost unanimously consider socialization to be the predominant factor in determining sex roles.
F 5. During infancy, clothing does not have sexual significance.
T 6. Parents choose clothing for their children to help groom them into future adult roles.
F 7. In our culture, male and female children are generally given about the same amount of freedom.
F 8. Because his socialization has been so thorough, when he enters puberty, the American male needs to make little change in his ideas or behaviors in order to carry on his sex role in the company of the opposite sex.
T 9. The term "puberty shock" is used to refer to an upsetting of the male's precarious sexual identity and the development of uncertainty about the taken-for-granted male/female boundaries.
T 10. According to this article, artificiality and manipulation become major characteristics of the male sex role in our society.
F 11. The author concludes that the American pattern of socialization into masculinity prepares males quite well for marriage.
F 12. This article is based on interviews with a stratified random sample of boys aged 11 to 16.

III. Essay

1. Describe the socialization process by which males in our society become "masculine."
2. This article describes typical reactions of boys to "sissies." What are those reactions, and what do they have to do with male sexuality?
3. Explain briefly the significance and importance for males of the socially constructed, semi-imaginary world of boxing, wrestling, basketball, football, etc., into which many men retreat from time to time.
4. On the basis of this article, why is it that men often have a difficult time "genuinely relating" to females?
5. What aspects of the male experience is the term "puberty shock" meant to describe? What is precarious about the male's sexual

identity at this time?

6. In what ways do you think the greater amount of freedom (in space, time, play, and other activities) that parents give to their male children relates to later adult sex roles?

7. Try to design an alternative socialization pattern for males that would be more conducive to satisfactory heterosexual relation- ships, one that would allow males to be more genuinely empathetic with the problems of women.

Article 12: Thorne and Luria, "Sexuality and Gender"

I. Multiple-Choice

1. To gather their data, Thorne and Luria studied:
   a. three- and four-year-olds in a private preschool
   b. third and fourth graders   c. children of Samoa
   d. nineteenth and twentieth century portrayals of children in literature

2. Boys controlling some areas of a playground, and girls controlling other areas, is an example of what the authors call gender _____:
   a. confusion   b. segregation   c. desensitization
   d. ramification

3. In general, when children are allowed to construct their own activities there is more:
   a. role ambivalence   b. gender integration
   c. gender segregation   d. aggressive behavior

4. The authors found that schoolchildren flaunting dirty words and risking punishment for their use is:
   a. more common now than during the 1970s
   b. less common now than during the 1970s
   c. more frequent in boy's groups
   d. more frequent in girl's groups

5. The authors report that the following are interconnected:
   a. dirty words, sex, and drugs
   b. dirty words, sports, and alcohol
   c. dirty words, alcohol, and sex
   d. dirty words, transgression of politeness, and sports

6. Which group seems to believe more in rules?
   a. Midwesterners   b. Southerners   c. boys   d. girls

7. The girls in Thorne's and Luria's study were most likely to organize themselves into:
   a. dyads   b. large groups   c. groups of six to eight
   d. social clubs

8. The authors report that, compared with boys, play among girls is more likely to involve:
   a. team sports   b. violation of adult norms
   c. synchronized body rituals   d. physical aggression

9. Compared with boys, the sexually related discourse of girls is

more likely to focus on:
a. dirty words   b. unanticipated pregnancy   c. growing up
<u>d</u>. themes of romance

10. Cross-gender games of "chase and kiss" are likely to result in:
a. interference from parents   <u>b</u>. girls kissing boys
c. boys kissing girls
d. dyads splitting off to play other kissing games

II. True-False

T 1. The authors report that the world of children is a microcosm of the larger adult world.
F 2. The researchers conclude that the play of children does not have serious sociological meaning.
F 3. Boys tend to be more concerned with intimacy, emotionality, and romance, while girls tend to be more concerned with sexuality.
F 4. The daily lives of children in elementary school have very few activities or encounters that are gender segregated.
T 5. The authors indicate that gender segregation in elementary and middle schools is more common than segregation by race.
F 6. Compared with boys, girls tend to interact in larger groups.
F 7. Compared with boys, girls are more likely to find group support for repeated public transgression.
F 8. Fifth grade boys touch one another frequently and with ease; they often place their arms around one another's shoulders, hug, and hold hands.
T 9. Girls are less likely than boys to organize themselves into team sports.
T 10. Compared with boys, girls are more focused on constructing intimacy and talking about one-to-one relationships.

III. Essay

1. How do gender divisions during the elementary and middle school years affect relationships between the sexes during adolescence?
2. How do boys and girls organize their play differently?
3. Contrast boys' and girls' groups in breaking rules and testing limits.
4. Comment on this statement: "The everyday worlds of boys and girls are a microcosm of the adult world."

Article 13: Henley, Hamilton, and Thorne, "Womanspeak and Manspeak"

I. Multiple-Choice

1. The use of the generic "he" in the English language is an example of:
a. grammatical reconstruction   b. generic replication
<u>c</u>. how our language ignores females
d. distinguishing characteristics

2. The authors say that the use of female names and pronouns in reference to material objects such as cars or boats is a way of expressing:
<u>a</u>. possession   b. pride   c. disdain   d. endearment

3. Words such as "queen," "madam," and "dame," which have acquired debased meanings, are examples of:
   a. how Americans frown upon aristocracy
   b. how the English language ignores females
   c. self-disclosure
   d. the deprecation of women in the English language

4. The authors say that this group discloses more personal information to others:
   a. men   b. sociologists   c. psychologists   d. women

5. According to the authors, which has more impact on our actions and reactions?
   a. nonverbal communication   b. verbal threats
   c. written language   d. pictures

6. The authors say that this group is better at interpreting nonverbal signals:
   a. Indians   b. Blacks   c. Whites   d. Asians

7. The somewhat tenser postures of females are said to convey:
   a. submissive attitudes   b. suspicion   c. anger
   d. a sense of self-importance

8. Which of the following do the authors identify as a status and dominance signal for human and animal groups:
   a. bearing offspring   b. bringing food to the nest
   c. touching   d. exchanging possessions

II. True-False

T 1. The communication patterns we learn as children help to maintain male dominance.
F 2. The authors found no difference between male and female speech styles.
T 3. Language both reflects and shapes the culture in which it is embedded.
F 4. More men choose to enter female-typed occupations than women choose to enter male-typed occupations.
T 5. According to the authors, a woman's sex is treated as though it were the most salient characteristic of her being.
T 6. Researchers found 220 terms for a sexually promiscuous woman, but only 22 terms for a sexually promiscuous man.
T 7. One researcher suggests that among the couples she studied, the conversations were under male control, but were mainly produced by female work.
F 8. Compared with their subordinates, superiors in work settings are more likely to self-disclose.
T 9. The authors report that women are generally more sensitive than men to nonverbal cues.
T 10. The authors say that, like other subordinate persons, for women smiling has become a nervous habit.

III. Essay

1. What significance does touching play in relationships? How does status affect touching?
2. In what three ways does the English language show sexism? Briefly explain each.
3. How do sex role expectations influence nonverbal communication? The use of space?
4. Explain the role of language in defining women as possessions.
5. How can self-disclosure encourage unequal status?
6. Provide examples of how nonverbal communication is sexist.

Article 14: Snyder, "Self-Fulfilling Stereotypes"

I. Multiple-Choice

1. An experiment by Mark Snyder, Elizabeth Decker Tanke, and Ellen Berscheid showed that men who were becoming acquainted with a woman over the telephone:
   a. behaved coldly if they believed the woman they were speaking to was unattractive
   b. were not as likely to ask for a date as those who were introduced to a woman by a friend
   c. responded more to the tone of the woman's voice than to what she was saying
   d. were fairly good judges of a woman's appearance based on the woman's tone and voice

2. In an experiment at Stanford University, women were given pictures of men they were to talk to on the telephone. During the ensuing telephone conversation:
   a. most of the women treated the men the same, regardless of their presumed appearance
   b. unattractive women were friendlier and warmer
   c. many women treated the men according to their presumed physical attractions
   d. attractive women were friendlier and warmer

3. Women who thought that a job interviewer held traditional views about the ideal woman:
   a. resented the interviewer's stereotypes and behaved coldly during the interview
   b. made the interviewer uncomfortable by challenging his views
   c. refused to show up for the interview
   d. dressed and acted according to traditional feminine stereotypes

4. A study of interracial job interviews showed that white interviewers:
   a. went out of their way to make black job candidates feel comfortable and relaxed
   b. were more prejudiced against black females than black males
   c. tried to make blacks look bad
   d. were less friendly and more reserved with blacks than with whites

5. Studies of interracial interaction suggest that stereotypes:
   a. are more prevalent in Southern universities
   b. may cause both blacks and whites to behave in accordance with

those stereotypes
c. affect whites more than blacks
d. affect blacks more than whites

6. The rewriting of Betty's biography demonstrates how:
   a. stereotypes influence male-female relationships
   b. stereotypes reinforce racial prejudice and bigotry
   c. people respond to nonverbal cues
   d. people reconstruct facts to support their own stereotyped beliefs

7. A management professor from Northern Illinois University told a welding instructor in a vocational training center that five of the men in his training program had unusually high aptitudes. As a result:
   a. the five performed better than the other men
   b. the other men resented the five
   c. the five did worse than the other men
   d. the five resented the other men

8. The study of mental patients by Amerigo Farina and his colleagues suggests that:
   a. mentally handicapped people are less likely than others to form stereotypes
   b. people tend to play roles that match the ways they think that others perceive them
   c. compared with stereotypes of race or sexuality, stereotypes about the mentally ill are harder to break
   d. I.Q. measurements are inversely correlated with the ability to form stereotypes

9. Regarding physical attractiveness and friendliness, researchers have found that:
   a. unattractive people are more outgoing and friendly
   b. attractive people are more aloof and shy
   c. unattractive people are less outgoing but more friendly
   d. there is little evidence that attractive people are more friendly and outgoing

II. True-False

T 1. According to the author, stereotypes are reinforced by the behavior of both prejudiced people and the targets of their prejudice.
T 2. The welfare of humanity depends upon the ability to generalize.
F 3. The power of stereotypes to cause people to confirm stereotyped expectations can be seen in male-female relationships, but not in interracial relationships.
F 4. A study of job interviews showed that white interviewers adopted an interviewing style that helped black candidates display their qualifications to the best advantage.
F 5. The author concludes that stereotypes have little effect on people's behavior.
F 6. Snyder found that the larger companies select personnel managers partly on the basis of their ability to resist stereotypes in their job interviews.

T 7. Snyder reports that members of stigmatized groups often
        subscribe to stereotypes about themselves.

III. Essay

1. Describe how stereotypes tend to be self-fulfilling. Give
    examples.
2. Explain the sociological significance of this statement in the
    article, made by a person who underwent a sex-change operation:
    "The more I was treated as a woman, the more woman I became."
3. Describe how self-fulfilling stereotypes work in employer-employee
    relationships.
4. Since stereotypes are so powerful, but are often beneath our level
    of awareness, how can we overcome them?

Introduction to Part V: "Social Groups and Social Structure"

I. Multiple-Choice

1. Which of the following is an example of social structure?
    a. interrelationships of the social institutions of a society
    b. the relationships between particular social groups
    c. how people are organized within some social group
    d. interrelationships among groups of nations
    e. all of the above

2. Which of the following is an example of a _voluntary_ association?
    a. one's racial group   b. one's friendship group
    c. one's ethnic group   d. one's family
    e. one's sexual group (that is, males or females)

3. Which of the following is an example of an _involuntary_ associa-
    tion?
    a. one's family   b. the YMCA   c. the Girl Scouts of America
    d. The American Medical Association   e. The Communist Party

4. The method of investigation by which sociologists directly observe
    what is occurring in a social setting is:
    a. interviewing   b. a random sample   c. the experiment
    d. a survey   e. participant observation

II. True-False

T 1. Neighborhoods, families, churches, clubs, and friends are all
        examples of what sociologists call social groups.
T 2. The social groups of a society are interrelated in various
        ways. That interrelationship is known as social structure.
T 3. To belong to a group means that one yields to others the right
        to make certain decisions about one's own behavior.

III. Essay

1. Define the term social structure and state what influence it has
    on people's lives.

2. List the types of social structure and give an example of each.
3. What is participant observation?
4. What is the difference between voluntary and involuntary memberships (or associations)? Give two or three examples of each.

Article 15: Whyte, "Street People"

I. Multiple-Choice

1. Whyte reports that goods sold by street vendors are likely to be:
   a. inferior to what can be purchased elsewhere
   b. stolen from "lost" trailer loads
   c. purchased by the vendor for resale   d. overpriced

2. The largest single category of street entertainers is:
   a. mime artists   b. music students   c. puppeteers
   d. jugglers

3. Whyte stresses that the following can have a strong binding effect
   on people:
   a. street entertainers   b. police officers   c. bag ladies
   d. vendors

4. Handbills are generally passed out:
   a. close to the potential point of sale
   b. to promote illicit activities   c. by advertising agencies
   d. to promote sports events

5. "Mr. Magoo":
   a. is a handbill passer   b. directs traffic
   c. sells hot dogs from a vendor's cart
   d. makes change for subway riders

6. "Knapsack man":
   a. passes handbills from his knapsack to passersby
   b. drags a knapsack along the sidewalk with bits of birdseed
      trickling from it
   c. uses his knapsack to slap the hoods of cars that are holding up
      traffic
   d. has a photograph of himself attached to a knapsack, along with
      a statement saying that only his family can assault him

7. Whyte says that shopping bag ladies have this in common:
   a. fierce independence   b. lower-class background
   c. low level of education   d. no family

8. How many residents of New York State mental hospitals have been
   put out onto the streets?
   a. 500   b. 5,000   c. 50,000   d. 500,000

9. The police hired Whyte to find out:
   a. which places prostitutes and drug addicts frequent the most
   b. which drug dealers also managed prostitutes
   c. the effects of police presence on prostitution and drug dealing
   d. who controlled prostitution and drug dealing within a certain
      area of the city

10. According to Whyte, the most undesirable criminals of the city can be found:
    a. in the subway world   b. at Central Park
    c. after hours in the nightclub parking lots
    d. near police stations

II. True-False

F 1. According to Whyte, bag ladies present a danger to others and ought not to be on the streets.
F 2. Whyte found that police ardently pursue street vendors because shutting down a vendor raises an officer's status.
T 3. Vendors use quick dispersal as a device to avoid confrontation with police.
F 4. Street entertainers are generally discourteous to those who do not give.
F 5. Street entertainers are known to brawl over prime territory such as the steps of the Metropolitan Museum of Art.
F 6. Handbill passers have a completion rate of about 8 out of 10.
T 7. The woman Whyte characterizes as the "witch" spits on little children.
T 8. Whyte observed a domino effect in giving to beggars, with donations coming in bunches--such as three or four in a row.
T 9. For his own big winnings in three-card monte, the dealer depends upon the player's taste for larceny.
T 10. Whyte observed that when the police appear on the scene of illegal activities, those activities cease during their presence. After the police leave, the individuals resume their criminal activities in that same location.

III. Essay

1. How does the quality of street life reflect the city itself?
2. What techniques do professional beggars and handbill passers use to get cooperation from passersby?
3. Briefly review Whyte's findings in the study he did for the police. Explain why this is so.
4. What does Whyte think about the presence of street entertainers and other characters? Explain why you agree or disagree.
5. Take a stand: "Our city streets have become more dangerous. The police have obviously lost control of much of the city. As one step in regaining control to make our city streets safe again, the police should vigorously enforce city ordinances against sidewalk vendors and street entertainers. Also, tougher laws should be passed against them."

Article 16: Henslin, "Trust and Cabbies"

I. Multiple-Choice

1. Which of the following is a criterion which must be met if a cab driver is to trust a potential passenger? The potential passenger must:
    a. desire a destination
    b. appear able to repay the driver in some manner for his services

c. appear that he or she will, in fact, repay the driver
d. all of the above

2. A cab driver is sensitive to misfits between "parts" of the passengers' fronts because:
a. his work forces him into contact with all social statuses
b. his success as a cab driver depends on such sensitivity
c. his life depends on such sensitivity
d. all of the above

3. Passengers with the greatest "trackability":
a. are "regular riders"   b. are "flag loads"
c. are "dispatched orders"
d. do not differ with respect to how they are located by the driver

4. Which of the following is least likely to be distrusted by the cab driver? The passenger who:
a. has a definite destination   b. is picked up at night
c. is picked up at the Greyhound depot
d. is picked up in a low-class district

5. Which of the following is most likely to be trusted by the cab driver?
a. white male   b. white female   c. black male
d. black female

6. Dispatched orders to cab drivers are:
a. always carried out by the driver
b. randomly selected by the driver
c. made compulsory at the dispatcher's discretion
d. This does not apply; no radio-dispatched cabs were studied.

7. The standard parts of "front" are:
a. setting, appearance, manner   b. setting, appearance, actions
c. characteristics, appearance, manner
d. face, clothing, cleanliness

8. The three standard parts of "front" were originally designated by:
a. Ichheiser   b. Goffman   c. Henslin   d. none of these

9. Which sitting behavior leads to the greatest distrust by the cab driver of the passenger?
a. in rear, behind driver   b. in rear, diagonal from driver
c. in front, next to driver
d. Sitting behavior is not one of the trust-distrust variables in the cab driver-passenger interaction.

10. According to Henslin, the cab driver's selection of passengers is largely based on a process of:
a. chance   b. stereotyping
c. collaboration with the dispatcher
d. bargaining with the potential passenger

11. The appearance of "trust" in everyday experience is:
a. prevalent, but rarely understood   b. recognizable, but rare

c. easily recognized and understood
d. easily recognized and understood by the more trustworthy people in society

12. The method by which the information for this article was gathered:
    a. questionnaires   b. a stratified random sample
    c. covert participant observation
    d. overt participant observation

13. The following is not a variable that effects the trust of passengers by cab drivers:
    a. marital status   b. age   c. sitting behavior
    d. residential area

14. The term "trackability" refers to the:
    a. ability of a cab driver to follow another vehicle
    b. public display of the cabbie license, with the cab driver's photo visible to the passenger
    c. tracing the writers of the bad checks that cabbies receive
    d. ability to associate a person with some origin of ongoing connections in the community

15. The phenomenon of trust has:
    a. never been studied by social scientists
    b. been studied only somewhat by social scientists
    c. been overstudied by social scientists
    d. been found to be of no importance to understanding human behavior

16. Cab drivers utilize stereotypes:
    a. in deciding whether to pick up black passengers, but not white
    b. in deciding whether to pick up both black and white males, but not females
    c. very rarely in deciding whether they should pick up passengers, relying instead on individuated factors
    d. as a regular part of their ordinary interaction in determining whether they should pick up passengers

17. Three important variables in the development of trust by cab drivers are:
    a. race, destination, and social class
    b. age, race, and religion
    c. social class, income, and literacy
    d. pick-up location, destination, and family name

18. The specific variables that lead to trust or distrust:
    a. remain fairly constant from one interaction situation to another
    b. change as the interaction situation changes
    c. remain hidden from the participants of an interaction situation until after the commitment of trust or distrust is made
    d. are obvious and often manipulated by the passenger as a means of taking advantage of the cab driver

19. To interpret the interaction between cab drivers and passengers, the author applies:

81

a. Ichheiser's paradoxical analysis of experience
b. Henslin's law of accumulation   c. inferential statistics
d. Goffman's dramaturgical model

II. True-False

F 1. This study was conducted in New York City.
F 2. Characteristics of passengers generally do not affect the cab driver's decision to pick them up.
F 3. In covert participant observation a group is aware that a researcher is in their midst.
T 4. Covert participant observation was the method used to gather the data for this article.
T 5. Blacks are generally less likely to be able to flag down a cab than are whites.
T 6. The "destination" of the passenger is often a significant clue as to whether the passenger is to be trusted.
F 7. The term "trackability" refers to the ability of a cab driver to follow another car.
T 8. "Trackability" is a variable that may refer either to passengers or to cab drivers.
T 9. Drivers usually trust dispatched orders.
T 10. Compared with moderately drunk passengers, extremely drunk passengers are more likely to be trusted by cab drivers.
T 11. The cabbie trusts very drunk passengers to a fairly high degree.
T 12. To a great extent, cab drivers operate on the basis of stereotypes in selecting passengers.
F 13. Passengers' ages have no affect on the cab driver's decision to trust them.
F 14. Cab drivers constantly deal with persons from all walks of life. They are also driving cabs in order to make money. Consequently, racial prejudices do not operate in making decisions whether to trust passengers.
F 15. Cab drivers do not refuse to allow someone to become their passenger unless they are afraid they will be robbed or killed.
F 16. Trust has been studied extensively by scientific researchers.
T 17. Trust is defined in this article as the willingness to interact with another person on the basis of the definition the other offers of himself.
T 18. The three parts of "front" are setting, appearance, and manner.
F 19. The three parts of "front" are clothing, gestures, and manner.

III. Essay

1. Relate "trust" (understood as the audience accepting as legitimate the offered definition of one's self) to events in your own life, in which you, as the audience, displayed trust. Also relate this concept to two events in which you did not trust someone. Specify the variables that affected your trust or distrust and analyze them.
2. Why do you suppose that race and social class are such important determinants in the process leading to trust or distrust?
3. Develop a fictitious interaction episode between a passenger and a cab driver in order to demonstrate the use of Goffman's concept "front," with its three parts of setting, appearance, and manner.

4. Apply the definition of trust as developed by Henslin in this article to other aspects of life in society (other social settings).
5. What insights into the cab driver's world were contained in this article? How could sociologists have obtained them by methods other than participant observation?
6. Should sociology concern itself with the study of such an obvious phenomenon as trust? Why or why not?

Article 17: Clark, "Sympathy in Everyday Life"

I. Multiple-Choice

1. The focus of Clark's article is:
   a. jealousy   b. sympathy   c. anger   d. resentment

2. Clark's three-part definition of sympathy includes:
   a. empathy, sentiment, and display
   b. love, compassion, and kindness
   c. suffering a loss, feelings of depression, empathy
   d. empathetic understanding, identification, and pity

3. The intensity of sentiment that a person feels depends on:
   a. how long people have known each other
   b. whether or not it is appropriate to demonstrate sympathy
   c. the degree of empathy experienced   d. a person's diet

4. Clark found that more sympathy was given to:
   a. widowers with small children than to widows with small children
   b. older women with car trouble than to younger women with car trouble
   c. thin people rather than to people who are overweight
   d. the destitute rather than to the wealthy

5. According to Clark, receiving sympathy:
   a. engenders resentment   b. obligates   c. stirs up strife
   d. is dehumanizing

6. The concept of "social margin" refers to the:
   a. social class structure
   b. social class divisions among the upper-middle class
   c. amount of leeway an individual has for making errors in social relationships
   d. ability to obtain credit, based on one's social standing in the community

7. Beyond the number of sympathy credits automatically "on account," a group member can obtain more credits by:
   a. negotiating them away from other players through shrewd strategies
   b. applying to the group leader for more
   c. making appeals to reason
   d. investing help and concern in others

8. According to Clark, the first rule of sympathy etiquette is that one should:

83

a. prove, beyond a doubt, that sympathy is due
b. never accept sympathy from a party more than once
c. not claim another's sympathy needlessly
d. share sympathy from one's own margin when another's margin is unexpectedly depleted

9. Clark points out that people who have their own problems are, to some extent:
a. exempt from the obligation to feel or display sympathy to others
b. absorbed in self-pity and don't require it from others
c. held responsible for their problems, and, therefore, do not deserve pity
d. expected to show more sympathy than others

II. True-False

T 1. Emotions do not just naturally flow out of us. They are conditioned by our experiences in social life.
F 2. The basis of this study is expressions of written sympathy in song lyrics.
T 3. Clark found that although empathy is necessary if someone is to be sympathetic, empathy by itself is not sufficient to produce sympathy.
F 4. Clark found that sympathizers are not influenced by people's social statuses.
T 5. Clark found that sympathy is a highly significant part of social life, that it can even mean the difference between going to prison and going free.
F 6. The term "social margin" refers to characteristics demanded by individuals from others in order to gain sympathy.
F 7. Clark uses the term sympathy accounts to refer to the more or less constant supply of sympathy that we can demand from others.
F 8. The number of sympathy credits a person possesses is unlimited.
F 9. Clark found that more sympathy is usually given to persons with chronic illnesses, such as arthritis, than to persons with shorter-term illnesses, such as pneumonia.
T 10. In general, someone who never claims or accepts sympathy from another over a period of time in a stable relationship may simply come to be defined as an inactive member of the sympathy network.

III. Essay

1. What does "social margin" mean? How does it apply to displays of sympathy?
2. Identify and explain the three major components of sympathy.
3. Discuss some of the rules of etiquette in the flow of sympathy in a given network.

Article 18: Henslin and Biggs, "The Vaginal Examination"

I. Multiple-Choice

1. This article is based on:

a. a sample of 12,000 to 14,000 vaginal examinations
b. a survey of gynecologists   c. a review of medical textbooks
d. the experience of physicians-in-training
e. interviews with patients

2. The transition on which this article focuses is:
   a. a girl becoming a woman   b. from patient to bill payer
   c. the historical change in role from doctor to bill-collecting
      business person
   d. from person to pelvis and back again
   e. from immaturity to maturity

3. The "lithotomy position" is:
   a. on knees and elbows   b. lying either on the right or left side
   c. lying on the back with knees flexed out
   d. sitting upright with legs extended   e. lying on the stomach

4. The doctor leaves while the patient undresses in order to:
   a. be more efficient and see other patients
   b. avoid the suggestion of a striptease
   c. fulfill the requirements of the Hippocratic Oath
   d. fulfill the requirements of the American Medical Association
   e. review his or her medical notes

5. Doctors are often embarrassed when their patients undress in
   preparation for the gynecological examination. To counter their
   embarrassment, the doctors:
   a. usually turn away from the patient
   b. busy themselves looking through the patient's chart
   c. almost always leave the room
   d. usually engage the nurse in conversation
   e. sometimes stutter as they help the patient undress

6. In the situation analyzed in this article, the patient usually
   does what as she removes her panties?
   a. turns away from the door   b. moves behind the table
   c. moves behind the curtain   d. requests a glass of water
   e. blushes

7. Whenever a patient in this study removed her panties:
   a. the nurse was in the room with her
   b. the nurse and the doctor were in the room with her
   c. she was alone
   d. the patient, nurse, and doctor made light-hearted comments
   e. the doctor turned his back on the patient

8. The dramaturgical function of the drape sheet is to:
   a. make the examination easier   b. provide a clothing substitute
   c. fulfill the requirements of recent American Medical Association
      decisions on gynecological examinations
   d. eliminate sexuality

9. The drape sheet hides the patient's pubic area from:
   a. the doctor   b. the doctor and the nurse   c. herself
   d. all of the above   e. no one

85

10. A major role played by the nurse in the vaginal examination is:
    a. bill preparer   b. chaperone   c. bill collector
    d. instructor in hygiene   e. dietetic adviser

11. The one who "plays the role of the object" is the
    a. doctor   b. patient   c. nurse   d. secretary
    e. receptionist

12. "My dress isn't too wrinkled, is it?" is likely to be asked:
    a. during the transition from person to object
    b. as the doctor is examining the vaginal area
    c. during the transition from object to person
    d. more by the younger patients   e. more by the older patients

13. The doctor is least likely to speak directly to the patient:
    a. prior to the transition to object
    b. during the physical examination of the pelvic area
    c. following the metamorphosis from object to patient
    d. who is behind in paying her bills
    e. all stages of the gynecological examination are about equal in
       this regard

14. Perhaps the chief concern of the actors in the dramaturgical
    examination is to avoid the appearance of:
    a. price gouging   b. sexuality   c. price fixing
    d. medical incompetence   e. lack of hygiene

II. True-False

F 1. The sample on which this analysis is based consists of a survey
       of gynecologists.
F 2. A major point in this article is that the conflict that many
       physicians experience between their role as healer and that of
       successful business person.
F 3. Male gynecologists often become embarrassed when their patients
       undress. To counter this embarrassment, most turn their backs
       on the patient while she is undressing.
T 4. Sociologists view clothing as an extension of the self.
T 5. As they prepared for their nonperson role in the gynecological
       examination, most women in the study hid their panties.
F 6. The drape sheet effectively hides the patient's pubic area from
       the doctor.
T 7. The dramaturgical function of the drape sheet is to eliminate
       sexuality.
T 8. The authors draw an analogy between the sacred and the vagina.
F 9. The longer a woman has been a doctor's patient, the more likely
       she is to undress in the doctor's presence.
F 10. The authors found that the younger patients suffered less
       embarrassment than the older patients. They conclude that this
       is the result of socialization into differing standards
       regarding the perception of self and sexuality.
F 11. In all stages of the vaginal examination, the doctors in this
       study avoided making personal remarks to the patient.

III. Essay

1. Specify how the medical personnel in this study of vaginal examinations avoided even the hint of sexuality.
2. "We live in a world of meaning" can be taken as a central point in the theoretical perspective in sociology known as symbolic interactionism. As delineated in this article, in which ways are events and objects dealt with in order to control (sustain or transform) their meanings?
3. Analyze the functions of the drape sheet in the vaginal examination.

Article 19: Schwartz, "Waiting, Exchange, and Power"

I. Multiple-Choice

1. A superior taking and making telephone calls when a subordinate is present for an appointment is best understood as a sign of:
   a. the heavy demands on the superior's time and energy
   b. the superior's inability to properly manage his/her schedule
   c. modern times   d. the subordinate's inferior status
   e. rudeness

2. The capacity of an individual to modify the conduct of other individuals and to prevent one's own conduct from being modified is a definition of:
   a. prestige   b. status   c. power   d. social change
   e. social interaction

3. The author states that, in general, these clients wait the most:
   a. northern as compared to southern
   b. southern as compared to northern
   c. public as compared to private
   d. private as compared to public   e. men as compared to women

4. The pattern of waiting practiced in American courtrooms most highlights the relative importance of:
   a. lawyers   b. defendants   c. police personnel   d. judges
   e. juries

5. In general, differences in the amount of time a person must wait illustrate differences in:
   a. social rank   b. subcultural expectations
   c. male and female socialization   d. education
   e. attractiveness

6. When Harry S. Truman was a U.S. senator, Winthrop Aldrich once kept him waiting for an hour and a half. After becoming President, Truman purposely let Aldrich "cool his heels" in a White House office. The author refers to this as an example of:
   a. punitive sanctioning   b. childish behavior
   c. exchange theory   d. retrospective retribution
   e. presidential prerogative

7. The author of this article compares time to:
   a. education   b. money   c. age   d. sand at the seashore
   e. leaves

8. A woman is meeting in her office with a male employee of the same
    organization. She receives a telephone call and says, "I'm sorry,
    I'm meeting on an appointment now. I'll have to call you back."
    She then terminates the telephone conversation. Having nothing
    else to go on, one could probably assume that the man in her
    office is the woman's:
    <u>a</u>. superordinate   b. subordinate   c. husband   d. friend
    e. lover

9. In this same example (as the preceding question), one could
    probably assume that the one who called on the telephone is the
    woman's:
    a. superordinate   <u>b</u>. subordinate   c. husband   d. friend
    e. lover

II. True-False

T 1. In general, the more powerful and important an individual is,
       the more others' access to that person is regulated.
T 2. In general, the more important a person, the more likely that
       person is to violate the terms of appointments and keep clients
       waiting.
F 3. Prestige may be defined as the capacity of an individual to
       modify the conduct of others and to prevent his or her own
       conduct from being so modified.
T 4. The less powerful wait more than the powerful.
T 5. One measure of the amount of privilege a person enjoys is the
       amount of waiting that person does.
F 6. Sociologists have found that one sign of the relative social
       equality of American society is that the wealthy do approxi-
       mately the same amount of waiting as the less advantaged.
F 7. In general, clients of private services do more waiting than
       clients of public services.
T 8. The author of this article analyzes time as a generalized
       resource whose distribution affects life chances with regard to
       the attainment of other, more specific kinds of rewards.
T 9. Far from being a coincidental by-product of power, control of
       time is one of the essential properties of power.
T 10. The control of time is unevenly distributed in the social
       system.
F 11. If a superordinate and subordinate are walking together, it is
       the subordinate who is the more likely to break the interaction
       and become involved in another activity.

III. Essay

1. Discuss why the powerful enjoy a relative immunity from waiting.
2. Discuss how time is a resource that is unevenly distributed in the
    social system.
3. Select some situations of waiting with which you are personally
    familiar and analyze it in terms of this article.

Article 20: Thompson, "Hanging Tongues"

I. Multiple Choice

1. The tongues referred to in this article are:
   a. people's tongues   b. dialects
   c. spinning records in the ghetto   <u>d</u>. cow tongues
   e. pig tongues

2. The assembly line on which Thompson worked was:
   a. an automobile assembly line
   b. the production of inexpensive furs
   <u>c</u>. the slaughtering and processing of cattle
   d. the production and packaging of SAT tests
   e. owned by the Mafia

3. The method of this study was:
   <u>a</u>. participant observation   b. semistructured interviews
   c. a random sample of plant workers
   d. a random sample of plant managers   e. the experiment

4. Working faster than the line allowed the workers to gain:
   a. a period of relaxation   b. extra pay (a bonus)
   c. symbolic control over the pace of their work   <u>d</u>. a and c
   e. the approval of the boss

5. Three main problems with which the workers at this plant had to
   cope were:
   <u>a</u>. monotony, danger, and dehumanization
   b. monotomy, dehumanization, and low pay
   c. abusive foremen, a sadistic plant nurse, and low pay
   d. abusive foremen, danger, and a weak-willed union
   e. boredom, anxiety, and heat

6. The main way these workers coped with the monotony of their work
   was by:
   a. playing radios   <u>b</u>. daydreaming   c. playing verbal poker
   d. telling stories about the foremen and cursing the management
   e. playing cards

7. To cope with the dangers they faced, these workers would:
   a. play pocket radios   b. carry large amounts of insurance
   <u>c</u>. dissociate themselves from those who were hurt on the job
   d. strictly enforce the "no alcohol and no drugs" rule at work
   e. often go out on strike

8. Daydreaming and dissociation with the injured were:
   a. severely frowned upon by the management
   b. severely punished by the management
   c. often the topic of lectures in the workers' monthly union
      meetings
   <u>d</u>. coping defenses used by the workers
   e. the cause of many injuries

9. According to this author, the assembly line is:
   a. a tool used by the worker
   <u>b</u>. a machine that controls the worker
   c. being replaced by computerization and robots
   d. overanalyzed by sociologists
   e. the key to our high standard of living

10. In a bureaucratic structure, when human needs collide with system needs:
   a. reeducation is attempted by enlightened management, oppression by traditional management
   b. unions become powerless   c. the result is innovation
   d. the individual suffers   e. workers are paid higher wages

11. When workers are seen as interchangeable parts, as mere extensions of the machines with which they work, according to this article the following is likely to result:
   a. dehumanization   b. strikes   c. malingering
   d. decreased production   e. injuries

12. When a worker would drop a piece of meat, he or she usually:
   a. looked around to see if an inspector or foreman had noticed and put it back on the line if it was unobserved
   b. picked it up and placed it in a tub marked "inedible"
   c. kicked it aside until he or she could momentarily outpace the assembly line and then placed it in the recycling tub
   d. was fined--the first time lightly, the second time moderately, but the third time (within any 20 day work period) he or she was brought before the disciplinary committee
   e. bought it at discount and took it home

13. Those who stayed at this job did so primarily because:
   a. they discovered a sense of belonging in the plant (a family away from home)
   b. they were caught in a financial trap
   c. they were high school dropouts
   d. their fathers worked (or had worked) at the plant
   e. of union rules

II. True-False

T 1. In general, the community felt negative about work at the beef plant.
F 2. The data for this article were gathered by semistructured interviews with workers and managers.
F 3. Although this plant was boring to work in, it was safe.
F 4. Whenever a worker was injured, because they identify with that person the other workers were highly supportive of the injured person.
F 5. Because they knew that their family and friends might eat the meat they were handling, if a worker dropped a piece of meat he or she usually picked it up and put it in a tub marked "inedible."
F 6. Unlike many factories, in this one the workers have high respect for management.
T 7. To gain a sense of symbolic control over their work, these workers often worked faster than the assembly line.
T 8. Three major problems that these workers coped with were monotony, danger, and dehumanization.
F 9. In general, these workers were highly satisfied with their work.
F 10. These workers tended to classify themselves into "new" and

"old" workers, and a "new worker" was ordinarily not given the higher status of "old worker" until he had worked at the plant about three years.

III. Essay

1. What are the major characteristics of this work setting, and how do they affect the workers' lives?
2. What is meant by dehumanization? How did these workers cope with dehumanization?
3. Most of these workers detested their work; yet they kept at it year after year. What constraints drove them to keep returning to the job?
4. In what ways do you think the work situation at this factory could be improved? Caution: Keep in mind the management's requirements of "bottom line," that is, their need to show a profit if they are going to stay in business.

Article 21: Coleman, "Diary of a Homeless Man"

I. Multiple-Choice

1. How many days did Coleman spend on the streets as a homeless man?
   a. 5   b. 10   c. 15   d. 21   e. 39

2. When Coleman wanted to eat breakfast in a coffee shop, what happened?
   a. some kind customers made room for him at their table
   b. the proprietor refused to serve him
   c. the waitress surreptitiously reduced his bill
   d. the counterman made him pay for his breakfast in advance
   e. a policeman chased him out, warning him to never come around again

3. How much money did Coleman take with him to see him through his adventure in homelessness?
   a. $0   b. $20   c. $40   d. $75   e. $100

4. One day Coleman read The New York Times. To obtain a copy, he:
   a. asked someone for it   b. retrieved it from the trash
   c. found it on a park bench   d. bought it at a newsstand
   e. read it at the reading room of the newspaper office

5. Aimlessly walking the streets in tattered clothing with no particular place to go brought this quote to Coleman's mind:
   a. "Idle hands are the devil's workshop."
   b. "It's what you wear from ear to ear that matters--and not from head to toe."
   c. "Idleness is only enjoyable when you have a lot to do."
   d. "You can't judge a book by its cover."
   e. "All work and no play makes Jack a dull boy."

6. Damage caused by drugs and alcohol was evident in:
   a. almost every street person Coleman saw
   b. about half the street people Coleman saw
   c. only a few extreme instances   d. primarily the young males

e. primarily the young females

7. After only a few hours of aimlessly wandering the city streets, Coleman began to feel:
   a. a useless part of the city streets
   b. a vital part of the pulse of the city
   c. free from the cares and burdens of life
   d. a sense of camaraderie with the homeless
   e. like trashing the stores patronized by the wealthy

8. The author's former occupation is that of a:
   a. priest   b. newspaper reporter   c. college president
   d. bus driver   e. fire fighter

9. Of the three people from Coleman's former life who made eye contact with him:
   a. each seemed embarrassed to see him, and said nothing
   b. only one offered money and assistance
   c. two acknowledged him, but offered no assistance
   d. one laughed in his face, saying he finally got what was coming to him
   e. none showed a hint of recognition

10. The man with the bullhorn at the East 3rd Street Shelter:
    a. shouted obscenities and insults at the homeless men
    b. politely assisted the men in any way he could
    c. slept on the job   d. was killed by a homeless man
    e. had only one leg and was barely able to get around

11. When a man made sexual advances toward him, Coleman declined. The man then:
    a. tried to stab Coleman   b. was evicted from the shelter
    c. pinned Coleman against the wall and searched him because he thought Coleman might go for a weapon
    d. enlisted a friend, and the two beat up Coleman
    e. apologized and said he had AIDS

12. Treatment of the men at the East 3rd Street Shelter might be best characterized as:
    a. outstanding   b. excellent   c. satisfactory   d. degrading
    e. constructive, especially in their efforts at job training

13. The shelter at the Keener Building on Ward's Island was an old, neglected building that still retained its atmosphere of the function it once served. What was that previous function?
    a. a meat packing plant   b. a mental hospital   c. a stadium
    d. a warehouse   e. a fish market

14. After Coleman went on the streets dressed as a homeless man, he noticed that people began to look at him differently. How does he describe this changed look?
    a. like hatred   b. piercing, like ice   c. full of compassion
    d. as though he weren't there   e. like mellowness and sadness

15. In 1983, 4,635 people in New York City sought shelter in the city's hostels. This compares to how many in 1933, when we were

in the midst of the Great Depression?

a. 524   b. 4,524   c. 18,923   d. 42,587   e. 129,311

II. True-False

T 1. Coleman found a place to sleep, a warm grate on 47th Street.
He knew about this grate because he had walked past it on his
way to work every morning during the preceding five years.

F 2. Coleman found that the faces of the homeless people he met were
more interesting than the typical faces on Wall Street or Upper
Manhattan, for they showed not only greater suffering but also
a deeper, more dignified character that had arisen from that
suffering.

F 3. The City Library prohibited the loitering of homeless people
who otherwise, seeking shelter from the cold, would stay all
day.

T 4. As he lived on the streets, Coleman soon fell into a set
routine.

F 5. Coleman saw a man selling drugs from a suitcase. Three police
officers immediately arrested the man.

F 6. Coleman found that, in general, the shelters for men were
clean, neat, operated by a courteous staff, and promptly
accommodated everyone seeking shelter.

T 7. A fight which broke out while the men were waiting in line for
lodging tickets resulted in one man pulling a long knife on the
other. The reason for this incident was the men's disagreement
about their proper place in line.

F 8. One night the men were not transported to the shelter until
2:00 a.m. (the Ft. Washington Avenue shelter). To make it
easier on the men, the next morning they were allowed to sleep
in until nine.

F 9. Coleman was most frightened by one group of men in the
shelters. That group was the large numbers of young, intensely
angry Hispanics.

T 10. Regardless of their age, race, background, or health, being
homeless and helpless tended to make men cow and passively take
whatever was dished out to them by the staff of the shelters.

T 11. The issue of respect and turf appears to be most crucial to
angry, young black males.

III. Essay

1. What causes of homelessness does Coleman mention? Can you add any
other causes?

2. What were the main problems that Coleman experienced as a homeless
man? How do you think the problems of a homeless woman differ
from those?

3. Speculate as to why the reactions of Americans toward the homeless
are so severely divided--ranging from deep sympathy and the desire
to help, on the one hand, to hostility and aggression, on the
other. Then suggest reasons that most people's reactions could be
classified as "verbal" sympathy that does not result in action.

4. Suggest how homelessness in the United States could be solved.
Don't neglect to be institutional in your answer; that is, don't
forget to place a focus on the institutions of our society.

93

Introduction to Part VI: "Deviance and Social Control"

I. Matching

1.	b. Appearance	a.	the violation of rules and expectations
2.	e. Conduct	b.	what one looks like
3.	a. Deviance	c.	crime
4.	d. Manner	d.	one's style of doing things
5.	f. Norms	e.	what one says and does
		f.	rules

II. Multiple-Choice

1. The norms that people develop to control one another include rules and expectations concerning:
   a. appearance   b. manner   c. conduct   d. all of the above
   e. none of the above

2. Another term for rules is:
   a. appearance   b. conduct   c. deviance   d. manner
   e. norms

3. Another term for norms is:
   a. appearance   b. conduct   c. deviance   d. expectations
   e. manner

III. True-False

T 1. Norms help to provide a high degree of certainty in what would be a chaotic world if everyone followed his or her own inclinations.
F 2. Deviance, the violation of rules and expectations, is not universal.
T 3. Hardly a single aspect of our lives is untouched by rules made by others.
F 4. As used in sociology, deviance is a term of negative judgment.
F 5. Deviance is another term for norms.
F 6. Manner is a term that refers to what people look like.
F 7. Manner refers to what people say and do.
F 8. Conduct is a term that refers to people's style of doing things.
F 9. Appearance is a term that refers to people's style of doing things.

IV. Essay

1. Deviants are people who break the rules, norms, or expectations of others. When someone becomes deviant, other members of his or her group react to that person. Discuss some of those possible reactions.
2. Based on the introduction to this section on deviance, what are some of the reasons that people react to deviants?
3. In what ways does deviance apply to appearance, conduct, and manner?

Article 22: Henslin, "The Survivors of the F-227"

I. Multiple-Choice

1. In what mountains did the plane crash?
    a. Sierra Madre   b. Himalayas   c. Andes   d. Urals

2. The survivors of the plane crash were from:
    a. Mexico   b. the United States   c. Canada   d. Uruguay

3. In order to survive, the survivors ate:
    a. snake meat   b. human flesh   c. seal meat
    d. raw bird's eggs

4. What did the young men on board the plane have in common? They
    were:
    a. medical students   b. members of the same family
    c. members of a rugby team   d. emigrating for religious freedom

5. It took days of deliberation and argument for the survivors of the
    crash to decide to:
    a. ration the chocolate and wine
    b. bury the dead   c. eat the corpses
    d. burn the wreckage in an attempt to attract the attention of
       search parties

6. What caused some, who had at first refused, to join in the eating
    of human flesh?
    a. the knowledge that rescuers were no longer looking for them
    b. the color and texture were more appetizing after the flesh had
       been cooked
    c. word from a priest on their short-wave radio that it was
       permissible under the circumstances
    d. they watched one of the children slowly starve to death

7. The survivors could eat as much of _____ as they wanted:
    a. snake meat   b. bird's eggs   c. human fat   d. chocolate

8. When one of the survivors set out to search for help, he gave
    permission to those who remained behind to:
    a. eat his portion of the chocolate and wine
    b. burn his belongings in order to keep warm
    c. eat his mother and sister
    d. use the remainder of his ammunition

9. After the rescue, government officials:
    a. awarded the survivors for their bravery
    b. kept the cannibalism a secret
    c. were sued by the survivors for not keeping the search efforts
       going longer
    d. named the mountain peak after the plane that crashed there, in
       memory of those who perished

10. After their rescue, the young men who survived the crash rejoined
    their families. They then became:

a. psychotic and withdrawn   b. celebrities
c. world class skiers   d. rescue workers in their own communities

11. Pick the false statement:
    a. For all of us, reality is socially constructed.
    b. It is possible to engage in deviant activities and to still maintain a "good" self-concept.
    c. In order to survive, all groups, including those that engage in deviant activities, must have norms.
    d. Unlike norms, meanings are not socially constructed.

II. True-False

F 1. All the survivors of the crash participated in cannibalism.
T 2. The plane crashed on Friday the 13th.
T 3. One reason that search parties could not locate the plane was because it was approximately one hundred miles off course.
F 4. The survivors of the crash were Hindu.
F 5. The survivors developed a division of labor based upon sex.
T 6. According to the survivors, slightly roasted human flesh tastes like beef.
F 7. The survivors made socks from the seat covers in the airplane.
F 8. After their cannibalism was revealed, the survivors of the crash were excommunicated by the Roman Catholic Church.
F 9. The survivors consumed every bit of flesh for nourishment--including the skin, head, lungs, and even the genitals.
T 10. Meanings are arbitrary.
F 11. The source of new ideas is not significant in determining whether or not they gain acceptance.
F 12. People's behavior has little or nothing to do with definitions of reality.
T 13. For their very survival, all groups must have norms.
F 14. Deviant groups, such as motorcycle gangs, have practically no norms.
T 15. Human groups tend to stratify.
T 16. Human groups tend to become organized.
F 17. It is not possible to maintain a "good" self-image and to still engage in deviant activities.

III. Essay

1. What rationalizations or justifications did the survivors use for eating human corpses?
2. Why do you suppose the survivors of the crash elected to eat the crew of the airplane first? Women and children last?
3. Why do you think the government wanted to keep the cannibalism secret?
4. Explain what is meant by this statement: "Our world is socially constructed." You may use the case of the Andes survivors to illustrate your points, but also provide other examples from your own experiences.

Article 23: Chambliss, "The Saints and the Roughnecks"

I. Multiple-Choice

1. The group of lower-class boys in Chambliss's study who were con-
    stantly in trouble with the law were known as the:
    a. Simps   b. Wimps   c. Saints   d. Rednecks   e̲. Roughnecks

2. The Saints' principal daily concern was with:
    a̲. getting out of school as early as possible.
    b. getting to school on time   c. getting gasoline for their cars
    d. staying in bed as late as possible   e. none of the above

3. One of the Saints, Jerry, was said to have failed to graduate from
    high school because he:
    a. was too "dumb" to graduate   b. was too lazy to do homework
    c. did not go to class as much as his fellow Saints
    d̲. did not "play the game" the proper way
    e. did not study as much as the other Saints

4. Both the local and urban police perceived the Saints as:
    a. poor kids   b̲. good boys   c. little heathens
    d. roughnecks   e. troublemakers

5. From the community's viewpoint, the real indication that the
    Roughnecks were "in trouble" was that they were constantly
    involved with:
    a̲. the police   b. girls   c. drunks   d. the Saints
    e. none of the above

6. The main types of delinquency the Roughnecks engaged in were:
    a. vandalism, theft, and drinking
    b̲. theft, drinking, and fighting
    c. drinking, fighting, and vandalism
    d. fighting, vandalism, and theft
    e. truancy, fighting, and drinking

7. The most obvious explanation for the differences in the reactions
    between the community and the police to the two groups is
    (Chambliss found, however, that the "obvious" explanation was not
    true):
    a. racial prejudice   b. one was a group of immigrants
    c̲. one group of boys was "more delinquent" than the other
    d. one group of boys was older and bigger than the other
    e. one group of boys had access to cars

8. Chambliss found that the simple reason underlying the differences
    in reactions by community and the police to the two groups of boys
    was:
    a. racial prejudice   b. one was a group of immigrants
    c. one group was "more delinquent" than the other
    d. one group of boys was older and bigger than the other
    e̲. one group of boys had access to cars

9. Part of the reason for the differential treatment of the two
    groups of boys was because the Roughnecks were more _____
    than the Saints.
    a. intelligent   b. affluent   c. peaceful   d. law-abiding
    e̲. visible

97

10. The group with greater access to automobiles was:
    a. the Saints   b. the Roughnecks
    c. neither had access to automobiles
    d. both groups had about equal access to automobiles
    e. at times the Saints had more access; at other times the
       Roughnecks had more access

11. From Chambliss's study, it is apparent that community response (or
    labeling) to deviance by the young is:
    a. in general, insignificant in its consequences
    b. highly significant in its consequences
    c. more important for lower-class people
    d. more important for middle-class people   e. none of the above

12. Of the two groups of boys, the _____ cut more classes, and
    the _____ did better in school.
    a. Saints, Roughnecks   b. Saints, Saints
    c. Roughnecks, Roughnecks   d. Roughnecks, Saints
    e. none of the above

II. True-False

F 1. The Saints were a group of upper-middle-class delinquents who
       were constantly in trouble with the law.
T 2. The Saints were highly successful in school.
F 3. The Saints never cheated on exams.
T 4. The local townspeople did not perceive the Saints' high level
       of delinquency.
T 5. Petty stealing was a frequent event for the Roughnecks.
F 6. The Roughnecks stole for thrills rather than for profit.
F 7. Unlike the Saints, the Roughnecks owned their own cars.
F 8. The Roughnecks' behavior in school was particularly disruptive.
T 9. Teachers tended to see a boy in the same way the general
       community saw him.
T 10. In sheer number of illegal acts, the Saints were more delin-
       quent than the Roughnecks.
F 11. The Roughnecks were truant from high school more often than the
       Saints.

III. Essay

1. In what ways did the perceptions of teachers and police (and
    others) influence the later lives of the "Saints" and the "Rough-
    necks"? (In other words, how did the self-fulfilling prophecy
    affect the lives of these young men?)
2. Why did their teachers and the police regard these boys as they
    did?
3. If someone were to use the terms "programmed for success" or
    "programmed for failure" (or "fated for success" or "doomed to
    failure"), how could you use this study to support or refute the
    ideas behind such phrases?

Article 24: Marx, "Unintended Consequences of Undercover Work"

I. Multiple-Choice

1. An undercover agent is less likely to vigorously pursue a target
    when:
    a. he or she begins to view the target with sympathy
    b. the target suspects the agent's true identity
    c. the target is involved in organized crime
    d. the pursuit might endanger a politician

2. Undercover agents develop a protective code of silence:
    a. broken only by police who are "on the take"
    b. similar to that of organized crime
    c. which they share only with a spouse
    d. that even lie detectors cannot detect

3. In his analysis of how street cops can avoid becoming corrupted by
    the use of coercion, William Nuir stresses the importance of:
    a. conversation and interaction with supervisors
    b. developing a sympathetic relationship with the target(s)
    c. following orders
    d. writing up detailed case notes to help the agent see things in
       perspective

4. Marx mentions this as a consequence of "playing the crook":
    a. an obsession with crossword puzzles
    b. resentment of one's spouse and family
    c. cynicism and ambivalence about the police role
    d. dropping out of church

5. New York City's elite narcotics force, the SIU (Special Investi-
    gating Unit), illustrates how:
    a. granting special authority to undercover units can result in a
       dramatic decrease in drug dealing
    b. administrative errors in communication can place officers in
       jeopardy
    c. moral corrosion and a lowering of standards may occur when
       agents are granted special powers
    d. much more effective law enforcement operations can be if they
       are not hindered by small budgets

6. The undercover California police officer who rode with the Hell's
    Angels for a year and a half:
    a. resigned from the force and ended up in prison
    b. committed suicide
    c. had to be treated for drug addiction before he could be
       reassigned to routine police work
    d. sued the police department for its failure to provide adequate
       backup operations

7. What is the major organizational problem of any law enforcement
    agency?
    a. overcoming the Peter principle
    b. how to screen officers for drug use
    c. how to supervise a dispersed set of employees
    d. training new recruits

8. "Going native," or becoming like the character that an agent is
    pretending to be, is particularly likely if the agent is:

a. a male   b. a female   <u>c</u>. cut off from friends
d. denied promotion

9. "Taking the devil's money to do the Lord's work" refers to:
a. the purchase of illegal drugs to alleviate suffering
<u>b</u>. agents using vigilante tactics against criminals, such as
    seizing drugs and cash
c. using drug money to entrap pornographers involved in the
    production of videos that exploit children
d. donating drug money to nonprofit charitable organizations

10. Marx reports that this factor increases the likelihood that an
agent will sympathize with the criminal he or she is investigat-
ing:
a. the agent's level of education
b. how many years the agent has been on the force
c. the agent's marital status
<u>d</u>. sharing age, ethnicity, religion, or gender with the criminal

II. True-False

T 1. The sociological principle discussed in this article is that
       people tend to become the roles they play.
T 2. It is not uncommon for undercover agents to develop feelings of
       ambivalence, guilt, and betrayal.
T 3. Some supervisors of undercover agents prefer not to know what
       their agents are doing or how they get the job done.
T 4. Some undercover agents begin to feel apart from, and superior
       to, other police.
F 5. Despite novels, television, and movie portrayals of undercover
       agents, they do not actually "cross over" to the other side.
F 6. Undercover agents are always relieved to shed their undercover
       identity and return to safer, less demanding routine police
       work.
F 7. Agents who have been undercover and who later return to routine
       police work are always regarded with respect and admiration for
       the sacrifice they have made.
T 8. The FBI's reputation for integrity and a clean-cut, straight-
       arrow image is attributable in part to J. Edgar Hoover's
       refusal to allow agents to face the temptations and problems
       confronting undercover police.
F 9. Undercover situations tend to be more rigid and predictable
       than routine patrol or investigative work.
T 10. Some agents have difficulty distinguishing their undercover
       identity from their real identity.

III. Essay

1. Why do some undercover agents cross over to the other side?
2. Based on this article, what steps can be taken to prevent under-
    cover agents from sympathizing with their targets?
3. What is the relationship between role playing and self-identity?

Article 25: Zimbardo, "The Pathology of Imprisonment"

I. Multiple-Choice

1. Which of the following does Zimbardo conclude is (are) a foundation for prison brutality and violence?
   a. the basic structure of the prison
   b. the type of people who are inmates
   c. the types of people who are prison administrators
   d. the basic personality makeup of prison guards
   e. all of the above

2. How were the subjects in this experiment assigned to one of two groups, prisoners or guards?
   a. by in-depth psychological tests and assessment
   b. on the basis of personal preference
   c. on the basis of their appearance   d. by a flip of a coin
   e. on the basis of their having criminal or "clean" records

3. The underlying motivation for the participation of the subjects in this experiment was:
   a. money   b. parental encouragement   c. peer approval
   d. a grade in a basic psychology class
   e. excitement and curiosity

4. How long after the experiment began was it necessary to stop the experiment and close down the mock prison?
   a. six hours   b. six weeks   c. six days   d. a month
   e. the "prison" was closed down at the regularly scheduled conclusion of the experiment

5. Four days after the experiment began, the experimenters had to release three prisoners. Which of the following was not one of the reasons for releasing them?
   a. hysterical crying   b. confused thinking
   c. severe depression
   d. extreme brutality against fellow prisoners
   e. all of the above

6. By the last days of the experiment, solidarity among the prisoners gave way to an attitude that can be summarized as:
   a. "Kill the pigs."   b. "We're all in this together."
   c. "Each man for himself."   d. "Catch as catch can."
   e. "I'll scratch your back if you'll scratch mine."

7. According to Zimbardo, the prison situation in the U.S., as currently arranged, is guaranteed to generate enough pathological reactions in both guards and prisoners to:
   a. debase the humanity of guards and prisoners alike
   b. lower the feelings of self-worth of both guards and prisoners
   c. make it difficult for either guards or prisoners to be part of society outside their prison
   d. all of the above
   e. Zimbardo says none of the above

8. The following is responsible for most prison upheaval and the violence associated with this upheaval, according to Zimbardo:
   a. creeping communism
   b. current prisons failing to rehabilitate inmates in any positive

way
c. "sick" prisoners being mixed with younger offenders
d. corrupt prison officals
e. the new liberalism that insists on attempting to rehabilitate people who are essentially incorrigible

9. According to Zimbardo, the seventy percent recidivism rate and the escalation in severity of crimes committed by graduates of our prisons are evidence of:
a. Prisoners are sick and incorrigible.
b. Current prisons fail to rehabilitate inmates in any positive way.
c. The prisons are doing their jobs.
d. The prisons are too liberal in their treatment and prevention techniques.
e. Prisons need to "toughen up" on these incorrigibles.

10. According to Zimbardo, this is one of the ingredients necessary to effect change in prison reform:
a. tougher guards   b. better enforcement of prison rules
c. tighter security
d. an increased budget for the state and federal prison bureaus
e. caring

II. True-False

F 1. It is apparent from this study that prison violence is primarily due to the type of people who are inmates.
F 2. The participants in this experiment were primarily ex-prisoners (ex-cons) and ex-prison guards (ex-bulls).
T 3. The guards made up their own formal rules for maintaining law, order, and respect, and they were generally free to improvise new rules during their eight-hour, three-man shifts.
F 4. There was very little change in the overall behavior of the subjects in this experiment between the time of its inception and the time of its termination.
T 5. No "good" guard ever interfered with a command given by any of the "bad" guards in this experiment.
T 6. A Catholic priest, who was a former prison chaplain, talked to the prisoners in this experiment and said they were just like the other "first-timers" he had seen.
F 7. Individual behavior is largely under the control of personality traits, character, will power, and other empirically validated constructs rather than social forces and environmental contingencies.
T 8. Zimbardo says that we all carry around in our heads a favorable self-image in which we are essentially just, fair, humane, and understanding.
T 9. This article indicates that many people, perhaps the majority, can be made to do almost anything when they are put into psychologically compelling situations--regardless of their morals, ethics, values, attitudes, beliefs, or personal convictions.
T 10. The mere act of assigning labels to people and putting them in a situation where those labels acquire validity and meaning is sufficient to elicit pathological behavior.

F 11. The experiment was terminated on schedule, about three weeks
       after it began.
F 12. This article demonstrates that people with sadistic personali-
       ties are drawn to the job of prison guard.

III. Essay

1. Describe Zimbardo's experiment. State the techniques that were
    used and the major results of the experiment.
2. Why was it necessary to close down the mock prison before the
    conclusion of the experiment?
3. Explain the process that turned college students into brutal
    guards, others into vindictive prisoners.

Article 26: Rosenhan, "On Being Sane in Insane Places"

I. Multiple-Choice

1. The purpose of this article is basically:
    a. to obtain an "inside" view of mental hospitals as seen through
       the eyes of patients
    b. to determine whether current practices in psychiatric hospitals
       can distinguish between the sane and insane
    c. to determine if normality is distinct enough to be recognized
    d. all of the above   e. none of the above

2. By presenting the pseudopatients' lives and past histories as they
    actually were, except for changes in name, occupation, and place
    of employment, the subsequent results were biased in favor of
    detecting:
    a. deception   b. sanity   c. change   d. insanity
    e. none of the above

3. Because there is little to do on a psychiatric ward, the pseudo-
    patients attempted to engage others in which of the following:
    a. conversation   b. note taking   c. card playing   d. chess
    e. planning an escape

4. All pseudopatients except one were admitted with a diagnosis of:
    a. manic-depressive   b. dementia praecox   c. schizophrenia
    d. paranoia   e. alcoholism

5. Of those pseudopatients whose sanity was detected, who did the
    detecting?
    a. secretarial staff   b. hospital administrators   c. nurses
    d. psychiatrists   e. patients

6. The data presented in this article speak to the massive role of
    which of the following in psychiatric assessment:
    a. testing   b. diagnosing   c. projecting   d. manipulating
    e. as these were pseudopatients, the experiment does not deal with
       psychiatry

7. Which of the following is a true statement based upon the informa-
    tion presented in this article?
    a. Diagnoses were in no way affected by the relative health or the

103

circumstances of a pseudopatient's life.
b. The perception of a pseudopatient's life circumstances was shaped entirely by the diagnosis.
c. The circumstances of the pseudopatients' lives did not indicate that they were psychotic.
d. The facts of the cases were unintentionally distorted by the staff to achieve consistency with a popular theory of the dynamics of a schizophrenic reaction.
e. All of the above are true statements.

8. Nursing records for three pseudopatients indicated that the pseudopatients' note-taking was seen as an aspect of:
   a. their pathological behavior   b. their innate curiosity
   c. their willingness to learn and understand
   d. their intelligence   e. their obnoxiousness

9. One tacit characteristic of psychiatric diagnosis is that it locates the sources of aberration within the:
   a. social environment   b. cultural environment   c. individual
   d. diagnosis   e. none of the above

10. For medical personnel to take a chance in the direction of sickness rather than health was described in this article as an example of:
    a. a tendency toward hypochondria   b. faulty medical training
    c. wisdom   d. a type two error   c. ignorance

II. True-False

T   1. There are a great deal of conflicting data on the reliability, utility, and meaning of such terms as "sanity," "insantiy," "mental illness," and "schizophrenia."

F   2. What are normal and abnormal are the same in all societies around the world.

T   3. The view has grown that psychological categorization of mental illness is useless at best and downright harmful, misleading, and pejorative at worst.

F   4. The staff at the hospitals in which the study was conducted was aware that pseudopatients had been admitted.

T   5. The choice of the symptoms reported in this study was determined by the absence of a single report of existential psychoses in the literature.

T   6. Beyond alleging the symptoms and falsifying names, vocations, and employment, no further alterations of person, history, or circumstances were made.

T   7. Immediately upon admission to the psychiatric ward, pseudopatients ceased simulating any symptoms of abnormality.

F   8. The pseudopatient, unlike a true psychiatric patient, entered the hospital with foreknowledge of when he would be discharged.

T   9. Despite their public "show" of sanity, none of the pseudopatients was ever detected by the hospital staff.

T 10. Medical personnel reinterpreted the "normal" biographical information of the pseudopatients to bring it in line with the diagnosis of schizophrenia.

III. Essay

104

1. Describe the purposes and procedures of Rosenhan's experiment.
2. What do the findings of this study indicate about mental illness and the medical profession?
3. Based on this article, what would you say is wrong with the psychiatric profession and the ways in which we treat mental patients?

Introduction to Part VII: "Social Inequality"

I. Multiple-Choice

1. Which of the following is <u>not</u> one of the broad bases of social class membership in our society?
   a. income   b. education   <u>c</u>. leisure   d. occupation
   e. the above are the four major bases

2. The upper-lower class is also known as:
   a. the leisure class   b. the professional class
   <u>c</u>. the working class   d. the "class"
   e. the "down and out" class

3. According to Marxist theory, the only thing that matters in determining social class is:
   a. the amount of one's education   <u>b</u>. the source of one's income
   c. the prestige of one's occupation   d. one's social heritage
   e. none of the above

4. The primary significance of social inequality is that it determines one's:
   a. prestige   b. occupation   c. wealth   <u>d</u>. life chances
   e. education

5. This term is equivalent to social inequality:
   a. income   b. occupation   c. education
   <u>d</u>. social stratification   e. none of the above

6. The main difference that distinguishes the upper-upper class from the lower-upper class is:
   a. the higher prestige of their occupations
   <u>b</u>. the greater time they have had their wealth
   c. their greater leisure
   d. their higher educational attainments   e. none of the above

7. This term refers to the probabilities as to the fate one may expect in life:
   a. educational structure   b. social endowment
   c. genetic endowment   d. social heritage   <u>e</u>. life chances

8. To be a member of this social class requires that one has had one's money for a long time:
   <u>a</u>. upper-upper   b. lower-upper   c. upper-middle
   d. lower-middle

9. Physicians, professors, lawyers, dentists, pharmacists, and clergy

are generally members of this social class:
a. upper-upper   b. lower-upper   c. upper-middle
d. lower-middle

10. The following social class is also known as the working class:
a. upper-middle   b. lower-middle   c. upper-lower
d. lower-lower

11. Blue-collar workers who work as seasonal jobs are usually members
of this class:
a. upper-middle   b. lower-middle   c. upper-lower
d. lower-lower

12. Most office workers in a local automobile dealership would be
members of this class:
a. upper-middle   b. lower-middle   c. upper-lower
d. lower-lower

13. Executives of a major manufacturing concern who have an annual
income of several hundred thousand dollars (and stock options and
bonuses may push their income to over a million dollars in some
years) are generally members of this social class:
a. upper-upper   b. lower-upper   c. upper-middle
d. lower-middle

14. A mechanic who repairs customers' cars in a local automobile
agency is probably a member of this social class:
a. upper-middle   b. lower-middle   c. upper-lower
d. lower-lower

15. A husband and wife who own a successful automobile agency are
ordinarily members of this social class:
a. upper-upper   b. lower-upper   c. upper-middle
d. lower-middle

16. Window washers and janitors who are hired by a local automobile
dealership during the busy season and are then laid off during the
slack season would ordinarily be members of this social class:
a. upper-middle   b. lower-middle   c. upper-lower
d. lower-lower

17. The social classes that are the most difficult to distinguish from
one another are:
a. the lower-upper and the upper-middle
b. the upper-middle and the lower-middle
c. the lower-middle and the upper-lower
d. the upper-lower and the lower-lower

18. "Detail men" or "detail women," those who make used cars appear
newer by washing and polishing them, painting their tires and
floor mats and so on, employed at a local automobile agency year
around, are generally members of this social class:
a. upper-middle   b. lower-middle   c. upper-lower
d. lower-lower

19. The view in sociology that says that to understand social inequal-

ity one need focus only on income is called:
a. the critical view   b. the corresponding view
d. the alternative view   d. the Marxist view

20. The probability as to the fate one may expect in life is called:
a. life chances   b. fateful probability   c. life probabilities
d. social causation

21. The probability of becoming the following is not affected by
social class membership:
a. being a drug addict   b. dying during infancy
c. getting divorced
d. all are affected by social class membership

II. True-False

T 1. All societies rank their members in some way.
T 2. The upper-middle class consists primarily of people who have
entered the professions or the higher levels of management.
T 3. Money is the single most significant factor in deciding a
person's life chances in our society.
F 4. Except for the socialist countries, all societies are characterized by inequalities between their members.
T 5. Social inequality is another term for social stratification.
F 6. The three main variables or factors that determine social class
membership in American society are income, education, and
leisure.
F 7. The working class is another term that sociologists use to
refer to the middle class.
T 8. The main factor that distinguishes the lower-upper and the
upper-upper classes is the length of time they have possessed
their wealth.
T 9. The members of all known past societies and every contemporary
society of the world are characterized by inequalities.
T 10. Whether a society's social inequalities are based on biological
characteristics, social skills, or money, the bases for ranking
are always arbitrary.
F 11. Systems of ranking people into different groups that are based
on social characteristics, such as wealth, are arbitrary.
Systems of ranking based on biological characteristics are not
arbitrary.
T 12. Social inequality and social stratification are interchangeable
terms.
T 13. If the son or daughter of a laborer goes to college and becomes
successful in business, that person has experienced upward
social mobility. Sociologists call this achieved membership.
If the son or daughter of a couple successful in business
becomes an alcoholic and ends up on skid row, this person has
experienced downward social mobility. Sociologists also refer
to this as achieved membership.

III. Essay

1. List the six major social class divisions in the United States and
briefly describe their major characteristics.
2. Identify the major difference between the lower-lower class and

the upper-lower class.
3. Identify the major difference between the upper-upper class and the lower-upper class.
4. What is the significance of social inequality for people's lives? (How does it affect life chances, which ones in what way?)
5. Present an overview of social inequality (social stratification) in the U.S.

Article 27: Domhoff, "The Bohemian Grove and Other Retreats"

I. Multiple-Choice

1. To what social class do most of those who attend the Bohemian Grove appear to belong:
   a. upper-upper   b. upper-middle   c. lower-middle
   d. upper-lower   e. lower-lower

2. What percentage of the fifty largest corporations in America were represented at the Grove?
   a. about 10%   b. about 35%   c. about 50%   d. about 60%
   e. about 80%

3. Domhoff stresses that the primary function of the Bohemian Grove (as well as the other retreats Domhoff analyzes) is to:
   a. provide a place of relaxation and recreation with members of one's own kind
   b. extend people's circles of acquaintanceship for business and political purposes
   c. challenge ordinary ways of thinking in order to develop fresh approaches for dealing with social problems
   d. integrate the wealthy from different parts of the country into a cohesive social class
   e. come into tune with one's inner self.

4. The hypothesis of this article is:
   a. People of all social classes need time for recreation if they are to continue to perform the social roles that benefit society
   b. The wealthy are pampered out of all proportion to their social contributions
   c. There is a ruling social class in the U.S.
   d. The poor are victimized by the social policies dictated by the wealthy
   e. Money can't buy happiness

5. Domhoff suggests that there is a ruling class in the U.S. He says it is made up of:
   a. the owners and managers of large corporations
   b. a conglomerate of the political elite
   c. wealthy politicians, businessmen, and entertainers
   d. top armed forces personnel   e. the electorate

6. The most wealthy one percent in the U.S. own what percent of all privately held wealth in America?
   a. 2 to 5%   b. 5 to 10%   c. 20 to 25%   d. about 50%
   e. about 75%

7. The wealthiest one percent of the U.S. own what percent of the
   privately held <u>corporate</u> wealth in America?
   a. 10 to 20%   b. 30 to 40%   c. 50 to 60%   <u>d</u>. 60 to 70%
   e. They own only privately held wealth

8. The view that the power structure of the U.S. consists of a wide
   variety of "veto groups" that form shifting coalitions to
   influence the decisions on national issues is known as the
   _____ view:
   a. veto group   b. shifting coalition   <u>c</u>. pluralist
   d. balanced allegiances power structure   e. commonwealth

9. The most wealthy one percent of the U.S. receive about what
   percent of the total yearly income of the entire country?
   a. 5 to 10%   b. 10 to 15%   c. 15 to 20%   <u>d</u>. 20 to 25%
   e. 60 to 70%

10. The author of this article says that besides journalistic
    accounts, the systematic evidence of attendance at private schools
    and summer resorts and membership in social clubs indicates that:
    a. the wealthy lead a life style different from most Americans
    b. the wealthy lead a life style that stands in opposition to
       traditional American values
    <u>c</u>. there is a national upper class in the U.S.
    d. the pluralistic view of the American power structure is essen-
       tially correct
    e. the country is doomed

11. Research in social psychology suggests that the best atmosphere
    for increasing group cohesiveness is one that:
    a. builds on common memories   <u>b</u>. is relaxed and cooperative
    c. increases tension to a moderate peak in order to increase
       alertness and mutual appreciation for the common tasks faced by
       the group
    d. places people of approximtely equal educational backgrounds
       together
    e. places the sources of tension in the leadership

12. At the end of this article, Domhoff stresses that this factor
    makes people open to the views of others of their group and more
    likely to change their views to those of their fellow members:
    a. similarity of education   <u>b</u>. social cohesiveness
    c. social dynamics   d. ethnic identity   e. gender solidarity

II. True-False

F 1. The Bohemians Domhoff analyzes in this article live a life that
     most consider disreputable. This is primarily because they
     shun the work ethic that is dominant in American society.

F 2. The High Jinks plays at the Grove cost next to nothing because
     no salaries are paid the performers.

F 3. The hypothesis of this article is that there is no ruling
     social class in the U.S.

T 4. Domhoff suggests that a social class made up of the owners and
     managers of large corporations rules the U.S.

F 5. The author of this article agrees with the pluralist view of
       the power structure of the U.S.
T 6. Domhoff is convinced that there is a national upper class in
       the U.S.
T 7. Research in social psychology suggests that physical proximity
       is likely to lead to group solidarity.
F 8. Research in social psychology suggests that groups seen as low
       in status are more cohesive.
F 9. This article demonstrates that the wealthy are not necessarily
       powerful.
F 10. To gain the data on which this article is based, Domhoff joined
       the Amalgamated Association of Waiters and "infiltrated" the
       Bohemian Grove.

III. Essay

1. Domhoff concentrates on social cohesiveness. To what social
    cohesiveness does he refer? What is the evidence for this social
    cohesiveness? And what is the sociological significance of this
    social cohesiveness?
2. Do you think there is a national ruling class in the U.S.? Why or
    why not?
3. Why do you think that Domhoff is disturbed about his findings?
    What are the implications for decision-making in American society?

Article 28: Gans, "The Uses of Poverty"

I. Multiple-Choice

1. The term for unintended or unrecognized position functions is
    _____ functions:
    a. reciprocal   b. retrogressive   c. latent   d. blatant
    e. limpid

2. The theoretical perspective utilized by this author is:
    a. functional analysis   b. retrogressive analysis
    c. conflict theory   d. the manifest perspective
    e. the latent theory

3. The observed consequences of a phenomenon which make for the
    adaptation or adjustment of a social system is the definition of:
    a. social change   b. functions   c. social movements
    d. society   e. adaptation

4. Which of the following is not identified by Gans as a function of
    poverty?
    a. subsidizing economic activities that benefit the affluent
    b. ensuring that society's dirty work will be done
    c. guaranteeing the status of those who are not poor
    d. offering opportunities for social (status) advancement
    e. all of the above are so identified

5. Society's physically dirty or dangerous, temporary, dead-end and
    underpaid jobs are referred to in this article as:
    a. dirty work   b. end jobs   c. the tough luck blues
    d. the lower-lower class   e. jerk jobs

6. Gans identifies restaurants, hospitals, parts of the garment industry, and "truck farming" as economic activities that need the poor to:
   a. function as consumers   b. do their dirty work
   c. act as go betweens between the producer and the consumer
   d. provide "fresh blood" for moving up the hierarchy of prestige
   e. receive contributions

7. According to Gans, accusing the poor of being lazy, spendthrift, dishonest, and promiscuous is an example of:
   a. punishing alleged or real deviants   b. a function of poverty
   c. justifying conventional norms   d. all of the above
   e. none of the above

8. The author suggests that poverty can be done away with by automation or higher wages and those who now serve the poor can expend their energies elsewhere (for example, social workers can counsel the affluent, and the police can devote themselves to enforcing traffic laws and fighting organized crime). These suggestions are examples of:
   a. dysfunctions   b. functional alternatives   c. functions
   d. preserving the status quo   e. fictional functions

9. The author concludes that poverty persists because:
   a. people don't like the poor   b. the poor are basically lazy
   c. the poor are poorly educated
   d. the poor provide benefits to society   e. people are poor

10. The author concludes that poverty:
    a. will continue unless functional alternatives are found
    b. is bad for society
    c. creates basic values that undermine the American work ethic
    d. ought to continue because it performs benefits to society that are usually hidden from view
    e. will soon be eliminated

II. True-False

F 1. Unintended or unrecognized positive functions are called blatant functions.
T 2. The definition of function is the observed consequences of a phenomenon which makes for the adaptation or adjustment of a social system.
T 3. Another way of saying "the functions of poverty" is to say "the benefits of poverty."
T 4. According to Gans, the poor are about as moral and law-abiding as anyone else, but they are more likely than middle-class transgressors to be caught and punished when they participate in deviant acts.
F 5. According to Gans, sociological research indicates that compared to the middle-class the poor are more given to uninhibited behavior (such as sex) and derive more pleasure from that uninhibited behavior.
F 6. Gans claims that one of the functions of poverty is the destabilization of the American political process.

111

F 7. The author indicates that, contrary to common assumption, the poor vote more for Republicans than for Democrats (although by only a slight margin).

T 8. The functional thesis of poverty is that poverty survives in part because poverty is useful to society or to some of society's parts.

F 9. The author concludes that because it serves so many functions poverty <u>must</u> exist.

F 10. The term functional alternative refers to something that, being a function for one group, is also a function for another group.

F 11. In this article the author basically accuses the poor of failing to take advantage of the opportunities offered them.

F 12. According to this author, the basic cause of poverty is the laziness (or, in some instances, a lackadaisical attitude) demonstrated by the poor.

III. Essay

1. Explain what is meant by this statement: The author of this essay did a functional analysis of poverty.

2. List five of the thirteen functions of poverty that Gans identified and explain why each is functional to society.

3. The author states that although poverty performs signficant functions for society, poverty is not necessary. If poverty were eliminated, how could those functions be met? (There would have to be functional alternatives for <u>each</u> function of poverty.)
   Granted this, can poverty ever be eliminated? Or is Gans's comment that poverty can be eliminated simply a sort of pie-in-the-sky desire; that is, does Gans's own analysis of the functions of poverty disprove his contention that poverty can be eliminated?

Article 29: Benokraitis and Feagin, "Sex Discrimination"

I. Multiple-Choice

1. The authors state that superficially courteous behavior, such as men opening doors for women, is:
   <u>a.</u> condescending chivalry
   b. making a refreshing comeback in American society
   c. a benchmark of civilized society in the same way as are eating with utensils and not cutting in lines
   d. not required if the woman has chosen to be addressed as "Ms." rather than "Miss" or "Mrs."

2. The authors say that referring to men as "little boys" or "little man" is:
   a. done primarily by women who resent male authority
   <u>b.</u> considered insulting, demeaning, or disrespectful
   c. a sign of affection
   d. a confirmation of male adulthood and authority

3. The authors found that a woman's marital status and whether or not she intends to have children:
   a. have no bearing on a woman's career
   b. have little bearing on a woman's career
   <u>c.</u> greatly affect a woman's career

112

d. affect careers in business, but not in education

4. The authors say that the belief that women should be protected may result in:
   a. women taking advantage of their kindness
   b. men doing their own work as well as that of a woman's
   c. men being reluctant to criticize women
   d. men jeopardizing their own safety to ensure that women are not taken advantage of

5. The authors use the term "dumping" to refer to:
   a. male employees dumping their troubles and problems from home onto their female co-workers
   b. male workers getting female employees to do a job and then taking credit for it
   c. using female guilt to get female employees to clean desks, make coffee, and empty ashtrays
   d. getting rid of older, less attractive female employees because of their age

6. Giving women directorships in dead-end jobs which are considered "natural" for women would be an example of:
   a. dumping   b. patrimony   c. showcasing   d. mainlining

7. The authors use the term "Queen Bee" to describe a:
   a. woman who shares sexual favors with men in order to advance her career
   b. naive neophyte or a woman who is insensitive to sex discrimination
   c. woman whose authority and status in the organization are strong and unquestioned
   d. woman at the pinnacle of her career

8. The authors state that new office equipment:
   a. is more suited for use by males than females
   b. helps female workers replace male workers
   c. may be dangerous because of long-term exposure to VDT
   d. is promoted by advertising that implies that it will promote office romances

9. The authors use this term to describe employers and employees who purposely and consciously undermine or undercut a woman's position:
   a. sabotage   b. exploitation   c. dumping   d. showcasing

10. The authors make the point that sex-neutral jobs that require professional or academic credentials:
    a. are the least discriminatory
    b. provide unusual opportunities for female advancement
    c. are often the most discriminatory
    d. make it easier to document cases of sabotage

II. True-False

F 1. This article focuses on racial inequality.
F 2. Subtle sex discrimination is by definition unintentional.

T 3. Gender is our primary identifier or master trait.
F 4. The authors support paternalistic protective behavior on the part of employers because it helps advance women's employment opportunities.
T 5. The authors say that chivalrous behavior, even though it may be well-intentioned, reinforces sex inequality.
F 6. The authors report that male political aides work harder than their female counterparts.
F 7. The term "showcasing" refers to the practice of placing young, attractive women in highly visible positions such as receptionists.
T 8. The derogatory term "Queen Bee" is used to refer to women in high places of achievement who fail to recognize women's issues.
T 9. The authors say that the hierarchy of a university might discourage office workers from taking college courses because it might lead the workers to wonder why they are performing high-tech jobs at low-grade salaries.
T 10. The authors say that one of the most widespread forms of exploitation is the use of female nudity in advertising.

III. Essay

1. Explain what condescending chivalry is and identify some of its intended and unintended consequences.
2. What are some of the ways in which women are exploited in the workplace? Give specific examples.
3. Apply the ideas contained in this article to some situation with which you are familiar.

Article 30: Fields and Fields, "The School at Society Corner"

I. Multiple-Choice

1. The events related in "The School at Society Corner" took place during:
    a. the Vietnam war   b. the 1920s   c. the Great Depression
    d. the Reconstruction Period

2. On James Island:
    a. few black people had money
    b. the dominant group was Cherokee Indians
    c. the main industry was the manufacture of baseball bats
    d. Irish immigrants were discriminated against in jobs

3. Society Corner school received its name from:
    a. its founder, Jonas Elijah Society
    b. the neighborhood society whose meeting house was nearby
    c. cynics who mockingly labeled it
    d. parents who were determined to raise the socioeconomic status of their children through education

4. The county intended to paint all of the schools:
    a. red, white, and blue   b. barn red   c. stark white
    d. muddy green

5. The teacher at Society Corner wanted the school and its yard to be attractive because:
   a. she took pride in herself and in her own appearance, and she viewed the school as a reflection on herself
   b. she wanted to win the contest for the most attractive school in the county
   c. there was no compulsory education in South Carolina, and she wanted it to look more attractive so parents would be more willing to send their children to the school
   d. maintaining the school's appearance was part of her job, and she was afraid that the administration would dismiss her on the basis of the school's appearance

6. Desks at the school at Society Corner were:
   a. donated by parents
   b. old ones passed down from white schools that had received new ones
   c. made by skilled carpenters who worked Saturdays fashioning them from the island's fine hardwoods
   d. modified fruit crates

7. The books at Society Corner School were:
   a. sent home with all the children during the summer months in the hope that they would become better readers
   b. not supposed to be sent home during summer vacation
   c. bought for use during the school year and rented on an "as available" basis during the summer
   d. used as rewards for students who helped maintain the school and the schoolyard

8. The first public library in Charleston was started by:
   a. Isaac Watts, a black educator
   b. Waldo Hamilton, a white author and newspaper editor
   c. Candace Clipper, president and founder of Daughters of the Confederacy
   d. Susie Dart Butler, a black woman who solicited funds from the Rosenwald and Carnegie people

9. In this article, "crackers" are identified as:
   a. black people who resented white participation in the predominantly black school's activities
   b. undisciplined schoolchildren who made wisecracks and disrupted the classroom
   c. white people who might set the school on fire because they thought it was too good for blacks
   d. people who broke the cycle of racism in Southern schools

10. The teachers found that some children did not attend the School at Society Corner because they:
    a. did not know it was open to them   b. lacked tuition
    c. were fearful that the teachers would beat them
    d. did not have shoes or a shirt to wear

II. True-False

T 1. The primary principle of functionalism is that various parts of society are organized to keep things running smoothly, each part contributing to the well-being of the whole.

F 2. A primary function of education is to teach students to question the dominant ideas of society so that through critical thinking they can restructure society into a better organization.

F 3. The School at Society Corner was heated by burning wood provided by the county.

T 4. When it came to furniture, the Negro schools in the county came last of the last.

T 5. Teachers at Society Corner were encouraged to purchase school supplies from Charlestonians, even if they could be bought cheaper elsewhere.

F 6. The School at Society Corner had 12 grades.

T 7. Mrs. Fields, the teacher at Society Corner, taught the children that black is beautiful.

F 8. The grandmother who attended night classes at Society Corner attended because she wanted to learn to write poetry.

F 9. It was the custom in South Carolina for newspapers to print the entire names of black people, Samuel Loen Roper, for example.

III. Essay

1. What were some of the obstacles Mrs. Fields encountered in starting the School at Society Corner, and how did she overcome them?
2. How did the fact that Society Corner was a black school influence its development?
3. What were some of the disadvantages black schools in South Carolina faced during the 1920s?

Article 31: Liebow, "Tally's Corner"

I. Multiple-Choice

1. The streetcorner man's low self-esteem:
    a. is largely a myth
    b. is due to the way streetcorner women are
    c. traps him in the street corner society
    d. is probably due to genetic failures   c. matches his abilities

2. The streetcorner men do not talk about jobs because:
    a. the jobs available to them are mostly the same
    b. they, too, accept the middle-class judgment of unskilled labor
    c. nobody ever has one   d. they don't like to work
    e. a and b above

3. The average man on the street corner can:
    a. expect to receive regular promotions if he applies himself
    b. expect to hold the same job for the rest of his life
    c. expect to be classified as an unskilled laborer the rest of his life
    d. look hopefully to the future
    e. increase his salary by harder work

4. The savings of these men are:

a. deposited in banks for safe keeping
b. in the form of portable consumer goods
c. hidden within their homes, primarily in mattresses
d. all of the above   e. nonexistent

5. The streetcorner men regard the future as:
   a. their only hope   b. the same as their present
   c. an indifferent matter   d. their enemy
   e. bringing worse things than the present

6. Highly paid construction work is:
   a. frequently beyond the physical capacity of some of these men
   b. highly sensitive to business and weather conditions
   c. located at such a distance from these men that transportation
      expenses become severely problematic
   d. all of the above   e. none of the above

7. These men come to jobs:
   a. with high hopes   b. wearied by the sameness of the work
   c. convinced of their incompetence   d. b and c
   e. expecting almost immediate promotion

8. The streetcorner men accept jobs that:
   a. do not push responsibility on them
   b. give them a prospect of success
   c. do not leave them on their own   d. a and c only
   e. will allow them to qualify for quick welfare

9. Streetcorner men often squander their entire paycheck in a
   weekend. Liebow says that this is because they:
   a. are childish   b. are addicted to gambling
   c. are so precisely aware of the future
   d. do not know any better   e. are very bad with figures

10. The employer's self-fulfilling assumption is:
    a. low wages for low ability
    b. a man will steal part of his wages on the job
    c. all men can handle responsibility if given the chance
    d. b and c   e. the men will eventually get ahead

11. Liebow pointed out several instances where the men failed to
    follow through on offers of good jobs; this he attributed to:
    a. lack of experience for those jobs
    b. strong feelings of incompetence
    c. fear of failure in positions of responsibility
    d. laziness   e. b and c only

12. The low-wage jobs at which these men work offer:
    a. hard, dirty, uninteresting, and underpaid work
    b. opportunity for learning or advancement
    c. a job worth doing and worth doing well
    d. peer approval and a fair amount of prestige in the fact that,
       if nothing else, he is at least employed
    e. opportunity for advancement

13. The streetcorner man reacts to his job:

a. diligently   b. as the spirit moves him
c. with profound gratitude for the opportunity to work
d. with hope for the future   e. with an eye to something better

14. The difference between middle- and lower-class time orientations
is due to:
a. a surplus of resources for everyone   b. different futures
c. psychological crippling during lower-class childhood
d. apathy   e. different sense of rhythm

15. The streetcorner man uses his money to live from moment to moment
because:
a. he has a short life expectancy
b. of the immense problems which challenge the human race
c. he lives on the edge of economic and psychological subsistence
d. he is immature   e. a and c only

16. Each lower-class man spends his money freely because:
a. his friends will borrow it if he doesn't
b. it is likely to be stolen
c. he is aware of the future and the hopelessness of it all
d. all of the above   e. none of the above

17. The attitude "I want mine now!" is:
a. greed   b. the ultimate cry of despair
c. a direct response to a perceived future
d. basically childish   e. not held by most of the men

18. Streetcorner men, if they work hard, can typically look forward
to:
a. a modest home in the suburbs
b. being promoted to a modest position of minimal respect
c. owning an apartment in the inner city
d. being broke and having a broken family
e. a relaxed retirement

19. "Long green" refers to:
a. the title of the book one of the men was writing about his
experiences in the ghetto
b. the nickname of one of the streetcorner men
c. the golf course these men sometimes play
d. a lot of money   e. the chance for advancement at work

20. In analyzing the effect of economic discrimination on black
streetcorner males, Liebow utilizes the following concept:
a. intuitive analysis   b. instructional analysis
c. self-analysis   d. self-fulfilling prophecy
e. neutralizations

II. True-False

F 1. This selection demonstrates that a man who is willing and able
to work can earn enough money to support his family.
F 2. Streetcorner men start a job with vigorous effort, but that
vigor is soon lost.
T 3. The only savings these people have are their portable consumer

goods.

T 4. A black streetcorner man's chances for working regularly are good only if he is willing to work for less than he can live on.

F 5. Wages are deceptively higher for these men's jobs because of the amounts taken out for dues to the labor union, retirement fund, and other deductions.

F 6. In streetcorner discussions, jobs are considered on their own merits and standards.

T 7. Self-fulfilling prophecies often keep lower-class men from succeeding.

F 8. Unlike the middle class, these streetcorner men have little or no deferred gratification.

T 9. For his part, the streetcorner man puts no lower value on the job than does the larger society around him.

T 10. The general attitudes, prospects, and life-styles are self-perpetuating in the streetcorner society.

F 11. Streetcorner men have reasonable expectations that their job will lead to better things.

T 12. What appears as a present time orientation in the lower class is as much a future orientation as that of the middle class.

T 13. The pawnshop serves as a bank for the streetcorner society.

T 14. Future time orientation collapses under pain or stress.

T 15. Dim prospects for the future give a general transient quality to daily life.

F 16. Generally speaking, the lower class welcomes commitments because they give value and purpose to their lives.

T 17. Being willing to forgo immediate pleasures for the sake of greater gains in the future is known by a sociological concept called "deferred gratification."

III. Essay

1. Explain Liebow's statement: "The job fails the man, and the man fails the job."
2. What is the banking system of the streetcorner man, and how does it work? How does this relate to his time orientation?
3. What effects might a guaranteed annual income have on black streetcorner men?
4. Explain the relevance or irrelevance of time orientations in trying to understand streetcorner men.
5. What is the self-fulfilling prophecy of these men? How does it affect their personal relationships, occupation, and life-style?

Article 32: Hughes, "Good People and Dirty Work"

I. Multiple-Choice

1. Some researchers are now substituting this term for the term race:
   a. color   b. creed   c. genetic pool   d. stock
   e. none of the above

2. The Nazi program of mass liquidation in gas chambers was carried out in the name of:
   a. reorganization   b. racial superiority and racial purity
   c. efficiency   d. resource allocation   e. overpopulation

3. One of the most significant characteristics of interviews with the German people after World War II was their reluctance to speak about:
   a. their loss of the war   b. prewar days   c. der Fuehrer
   <u>d</u>. the atrocities committed against the Jews   e. the future

4. Hughes states that the reactions of the German people toward the handling of the "Jewish problem" may be compared to the reaction in our own country by "all good people" toward:
   a. blacks   b. Jews   <u>c</u>. criminals   d. politicians
   e. professors

5. Which term best describes the feelings and reactions of the majority of the German people toward the handling of the "Jewish problem" by the Nazis?
   a. indifference   b. apathy   c. disdain   <u>d</u>. ambivalence
   e. unconditional support

6. In Nazi Germany the people who actually did the dirty work were members of:
   a. the German aristocracy   <u>b</u>. the S.S.   c. the bourgeoisie
   d. mental institutions   e. the unemployed

7. Top members of the Nazi party were found to have had a history of
   _____ according to those who have studied them intensively:
   <u>a</u>. failure   b. bronchitis
   c. extreme dependency on their members   d. mental illness
   e. perversion

8. According to Eugen Kogon, the Nazis came to power by creating:
   <u>a</u>. a state within a state   b. the promise of a heaven on earth
   c. a true democracy
   d. a childlike dependency on the part of the masses
   e. an economic boom

9. When Sighele said, "At the center of the crowd look for the sect," he referred to:
   a. the lunatic fringe   b. the religious sect
   c. the lonely crowd   d. the masses   <u>e</u>. the political sect

10. According to Hughes, the problem of _____ is one of the most serious in modern societies:
    a. the Jews   b. unemployment
    c. the German proclivity to accepting authority
    d. people who have no common sense (the lumpenproletariat)
    <u>e</u>. people who have "run aground" (those with personalities warped toward perverse punishment and cruelty)

11. The term that refers to destroying an entire group of people on the basis of their presumed race or ethnicity is:
    a. lumpenproletariat   b. inhumanity   <u>c</u>. genocide
    d. hitlercide   e. fratricide

II. True-False

F 1. The Holocaust, which occurred in Nazi Germany, was based at least in part on the fact that at that time the German people were poorly educated and were behind the Western world in modern technological development.

T 2. Hughes says that the National Socialist government of Germany perpetuated and boasted of the most colossal piece of social dirty work the world has ever seen.

F 3. The Nazi programs of genocide were aimed exclusively at the Jewish population.

F 4. The reason the Holocaust took place in Nazi Germany is that the German people had a race consciousness that became combined with their penchant for sadistic cruelty and an unquestioned acceptance of whatever is done by those who are in authority.

F 5. Pre-Nazi German society was much more racist than pre-World War II American society.

T 6. The Germans Hughes interviewed appeared to believe that in pre-Nazi Germany the good positions in medicine, law, and government were predominantly occupied by Jews.

T 7. The gory details of what went on in the concentration camps of Nazi Germany were kept a close secret from the majority of the German people.

T 8. Hughes suggests that the higher and more expert functionaries who act on our behalf represent a kind of distillation of our public wishes, while some of the others manifest impulses of which we are or wish to be less aware.

T 9. All societies of any great size have "in-groups" and "out-groups."

F 10. "Hitlercide" is a term that refers to destroying an entire group of people on the basis of their presumed race or ethnicity.

T 11. It appears that the greater the social distance we feel between ourselves and an out-group, the more we are likely to leave that out-group in the hands of others to whom we give a mandate to deal with them on our behalf.

III. Essay

1. Discuss how Hughes uses the concepts "in-groups" and "out-groups" to explain the apparent attitudes of the German people toward how the Nazis handled the "Jewish problem."

2. Explain what Hughes means when he states: "I think the study of militant social movements does show that these warped people seek a place in them." What types of "warped" people is he speaking of, and what types of "place" are these people most likely to seek?

3. Hughes states that "if the Nazi movement teaches us anything at all, it is that if any shadow of mandate be given to such people" (those who in his terms are "warped"), "they will--having compromised us--make it larger and larger." Explain the processes by which this might be accomplished in our own society.

4. Why do you think Hughes compared the Nazis and the Jews to prisons in America? In what ways is such a comparison appropriate? In what ways inappropriate?

5. Could events similar to those covered by this article happen here? Let your imagination go and specify conditions under which it would be possible.

Introduction to Part VIII: "Social Institutions"

I. Multiple-Choice

1. Which of the following could be considered a social institution?
   a. the family   b. religion   c. politics   d. all of the above
   e. b and c only

2. If the social institutions of our society were different, the
   following would also be different:
   a. our ideas   b. our attitudes
   c. our orientation to the social world   d. all of the above
   e. a and c only

3. The primary social institutions are:
   a. the economy, political system, and the military
   b. the economy, education, and political system
   c. education, the military, and religion
   d. the family, religion, and medicine

4. These are secondary social institutions:
   a. the economy, political system, and the military
   b. the economy, education, and political system
   c. education, the military, and religion
   d. the family, religion, and medicine

5. When they say that some social institutions are primary, conflict
   theorists are referring to:
   a. the first institutions to which an individual is exposed
   b. the significance of an institution for socialization
   c. the size of an institution   d. power

II. True-False

T 1. To understand a society, it is absolutely necessary to under-
      stand the institutions of that society.
T 2. Social institutions provide the structure within which inter-
      action takes place.
T 3. The characteristics of a society's institutions dictate much of
      the interaction of the people living in that society.
T 4. Social institutions establish the context in which people live.
      For this reason we can say that if the social institutions of a
      society were different the people of that society would be
      different; that is, their ideas, attitudes, and other
      orientations to the social world, and even to life itself,
      would be different.
F 5. Time is an example of a social institution.

III. Essay

1. Define the term social institution.
2. Nine social institutions are listed in the introduction to this
   section of the book. List seven of them.

3. According to the introduction to this section, how important are social institutions for people? What effects do social institutions have on people?
4. How can understanding the social institutions of a society be a key to understanding that society?

Article 33: Gracey, "Learning the Student Role"

I. Multiple-Choice

1. Gracey says that education is a _____ institution:
   a. primary   b. secondary   c. fiduciary   d. seditionary

2. Gracey identifies this as the unique job of kindergarten in education:
   a. reinforcing what parents have taught at home
   b. providing a creative outlet for children
   c. raising the level of children's spiritual consciousness
   d. teaching children the student role

3. Children who do not submit to school routines become known as:
   a. critical thinkers   b. gifted children   d. problem children
   d. late bloomers

4. In the classroom that Gracey observed, spontaneous interests or observations from the children were:
   a. never developed by the teacher
   b. immediately rewarded by the teacher   c. not expressed
   d. taken as a sign of keen intelligence by the teachers and administration

5. The classroom that Gracey observed is an example of:
   a. Montessori education as practiced on the West Coast
   b. Piaget's Progressive Education
   c. a typical class conducted by an experienced and respected teacher
   d. accelerated education based on Durkheim's concept of the "open schoolroom"

II. True-False

F 1. The educational system is one aspect of modern society that has not yet become bureaucratized.
T 2. The author takes the position that the main element of the student role is following classroom routines.
T 3. The classroom teacher in this article followed rigid routines.
F 4. The kindergarten teacher frequently solicited original ideas for activities from the children.
F 5. The school that Gracey reports on is an experimental school with few or little routines.
F 6. In the classroom that Gracey observed, when children were told to line up they were encouraged to ask "What for?" and "Why?"
T 7. The children whom Gracey studied formed informal, friendly subgroups in which they engaged in unofficial behavior.

III. Essay

1. In what ways do you think that Gracey's argument that kindergarten is boot camp is right *and* wrong?
2. Compare your own experience in kindergarten with this report.
3. If you were a kindergarten teacher, how would you do things differently?

Article 34: Roache, "Confessions of a Househusband"

I. Multiple-Choice

1. Roache concludes that the reality that lies behind the stereotypes of the nag, the clinging housewife, and the telephone gossip is:
   a. unfounded
   b. a lie made up by husbands to keep their wives subservient
   c. characteristic of only about one-fourth of wives
   d. a function of the role, not the person

2. After Roache began to perform household chores, his initial enthusiasm soon faded. This was due to:
   a. his wife's failure to notice his accomplishments
   b. his attitude that housework is women's work
   c. the repetitive nature of the tasks--constantly having to redo what he had just done
   d. not being as efficient as his wife

3. After Roache began to perform household chores:
   a. his standards of cleanliness fell rapidly
   b. he became neater than ever
   c. he became what he calls a "telephone gossip"
   d. he could no longer sleep at night

4. After Roache began to perform household chores:
   a. his standards of cleanliness fell rapidly
   b. he saw his insistence on neatness as a middle-class hang-up
   c. he became irritable and resentful   d. all of the above

5. Roache became angry with his children because they:
   a. were too noisy   b. messed up the house
   c. interrupted him all the time
   d. would not carry their share of the workload

6. During the months that Roache spent doing housework:
   a. his professional work flourished because of the extra time this gave him to be creative
   b. his professional work came to a standstill
   c. he grew closer to his children and was able to spend more quality time with them
   d. his careful planning allowed him to take care of the household responsibilities in about two hours a day

7. Before Roache assumed the responsibility of doing the housework, when his wife would express discontentment he would:
   a. try to buy her cooperation by giving her more grocery money
   b. hire a housekeeper   c. threaten divorce
   d. make her feel guilty

II. True-False

F 1. Most Americans expect their marriage to be about the same as their grandparents' marriage was.

T 2. According to Roache, sex-role privilege turns half of humanity into subordinates and the other half into their rivals.

F 3. When he began to do housework, Roache was surprised at how little there was to do.

T 4. When he was a househusband, Roache began to feel a sense of fulfillment through his wife's achievements.

T 5. Roache's experiences as a househusband helped him to understand how perception and personality become distorted as a result of being the "superior" in a hierarchical structure.

F 6. After Roache began doing housework, his communication with his wife and children improved.

F 7. In general, Roache found his experiences as a househusband satisfying.

III. Essay

1. Explain what the author means by this statement: "Only after I had assumed the role of househusband, and was myself caught in the 'trap of domesticity,' did I realize that the reality behind those stereotypes is a function of the role, not the person."

2. Why did it take so many years for Jan Roache to force a change in the arrangements that she and her husband had made for fulfilling the household responsibilities?

3. Explain the process by which the subordinates in a hierarchical structure become alienated from their superiors--and how the superiors end up with distorted perception and personality.

Article 35: Roache, "The Myth of Male Helplessness"

I. Multiple-Choice

1. Roache says that males who perform traditionally female tasks in television commercials, such as laundering or cooking, are portrayed as:
   a. more proficient than females   b. angry and resentful
   c. unsuccessful in business or career   d. incompetent

2. Excluding yard work and appliance repair, about what proportion of housework do women do?
   a. 20%   b. 40%   c. 60%   d. 80%

3. Why are most men not knowledgeable about cooking, laundering, and shopping?
   a. they don't want to learn   b. genetic programming
   c. women jealously guard their household secrets
   d. men do not learn these tasks as readily as women

4. Even though they both work full time outside the home, most men do considerably less housework than their wives. This is because:
   a. the long history of humanity has programmed women genetically for this work

b. men resist doing housework because it is drudgery
c. women don't want to give up this part of their traditional role
d. of interference by mothers-in-law

II. True-False

T 1. Roache says that he had to overcome his gender socialization in order to adjust to being a single parent.
T 2. Roache says that househusbands have become almost commonplace, appearing regularly in the style sections of newspapers all over the country.
F 3. Although the finding has created extreme controversy, researchers have found that female genes carry more homemaking traits.
F 4. Roache makes the point that the average husband of a wife who works full time outside the home now does almost half the housework.
F 5. Roache uses the controversial finding that women are more genetically programmed for household tasks to explain the fact that most husbands do less housework than their wives.

III. Essay

1. Why can't we be certain now just how we will play the role of husband or wife in the future?
2. Explain how the myth of male helplessness perpetuates female drudgery.
3. How do stereotypes in advertising help perpetuate the myth of male helplessness?
4. With all the ideas of equality of the sexes that American youth subscribe to, one would think that people getting married now would divide household tasks about equally. Recent studies, however, show that little has changed in the division of housework since Roache wrote his article: Husbands still do considerably less housework than their wives--even though both work full time outside the home. Why do you think this is so? Explain how Roache's analysis helps us understand this. What other factors may be at work?

Article 36: Hong and Dearman, "The Streetcorner Preacher"

I. Multiple-Choice

1. Most passers-by regard streetcorner preachers as:
    a. crazy   b. hard-hearted   c. awe-inspiring   d. disgusting

2. Streetcorner preachers regard passers-by as:
    a. victims   b. disgusting   c. sinners   d. hard-hearted

3. The authors concluded that streetcorner preachers were:
    a. crazy   b. content   c. acting out their need for attention
    d. rational, intelligent, sincere, dedicated Christians

4. The social organization of these streetcorner preachers is mani-
    fested in their:
    a. informal status hierarchy   b. concern over territoriality

c. church salaries   <u>d</u>. a and b only

5. When they preach, these streetcorner preachers are emotional and their utterances are disjunct (not logically connected). When they engage in social talks, they:
   a. are emotional and their utterances are disjunct
   b. are emotional, but their utterances are coherent
   c. are much less emotional, but their utterances are disjunct
   <u>d</u>. speak conventionally and coherently

6. During coffee breaks, these streetcorner preachers usually speak about:
   a. their sinful past
   <u>b</u>. a wide variety of subjects, ranging from politics to personal events
   c. almost any topic but religion   d. almost no topic but religion

7. The major factor that appears to keep these streetcorner preachers away from the mainstream of the ministry is:
   <u>a</u>. because they have no congregation, they cannot get a pastoral appointment
   b. the streetcorner preachers see street preaching as their vocation
   c. the streetcorner preachers look down on regular pastors, viewing them as avoiding the hard work
   d. the mainstream ministry offers too little salary

8. These streetcorner preachers:
   a. have little education
   b. do not develop logical, coherent messages, but are intent on "sowing seeds" that might later take root
   c. direct most of their efforts to the immediate conversion of whoever will listen to them
   <u>d</u>. a and b only

9. Status differentiation in the informal status hierarchy of these streetcorner preachers is determined by:
   <u>a</u>. the style of the preacher's delivery
   b. their use of the term "reverend" in addressing some, but "pastor" and "preacher" in addressing others
   c. the presence or absence of ordination   d. a and b only

10. When a representative of a rival religious group tries to take over the corner on which these preachers preach, these street-corner preachers:
    <u>a</u>. join ranks and move close to the intruder, shouting their message
    b. ask the intruder to leave; if he (she) will not, they call on help from the police
    c. complain to the supervisor of the intruder
    d. ask the intruder to leave; if he (she) will not, they take his (her) literature and warn him (her) not to show up again or else "things will get worse"

II. True-False

F 1. These streetcorner preachers were licensed and ordained by their church, and the streetcorner was, in effect, their pulpit.
F 2. These streetcorner preachers are disorganized, and it is difficult to predict just when they will show up on the street to preach.
F 3. These streetcorner preachers are quite jealous of one another's preaching skills and the attention others receive. Accordingly, even though they share denominational membership, they feel isolated from one another and have little to do with one another during their "breaks" from preaching.
T 4. Rather than attempting to deliver a coherent, logical discourse, the streetcorner preachers are intent on "sowing seeds."
F 5. The primary concern of these streetcorner preachers is the immediate conversion of whoever will listen to them.
T 6. These streetcorner preachers have an informal status hierarchy, in which status differentiation is determined by the style of delivery and paraphernalia of the preachers.
F 7. During informal social conversations, one of the favorite topics of these streetcorner preachers is their life before conversion.
F 8. The researchers found that about two of every three of these streetcorner preachers had gone through the spiritual conversion experience of "rebirth."
F 9. Most of these men were college dropouts.
F 10. Because they see street preaching as their vocation, most of these men are not interested in conducting religious services in church.
F 11. Street preaching is a stepping-stone for advancing toward a pastoral appointment.

III. Essay

1. Why do you think the ideas of typical passers-by and those of the streetcorner preachers are likely to differ so much? State those differences, and provide evidence from the article to support your suggestions as to why they differ.
2. Characterize the streetcorner preachers according to their (a) education, (b) past life, (c) social organization, (d) purpose, as they see it, and (e) relationship to the denomination to which they belong.
3. What are your attitudes toward streetcorner preachers? Use this article to explain your attitude.

Article 37: Lyng, "Edgework"

I. Multiple-Choice

1. People who do "edgework":
   a. require order in their lives; they need to keep the "edges" straight by constantly putting things in order
   b. desire an element of danger, and want to test the outer limits of their ability to cope with dangerous situations
   c. are assigned menial, marginal labor in society
   d. are considered to be on the cutting edge of their occupations

because of their qualifications in state-of-the-art technical advancements in their work

2. Lyng used participant observation to collect data on the world of:
   a. fire fighters   b. drug dealers   c. tax accountants
   d. skydivers

3. People who do edgework are involved in activities that most people would regard as:
   a. demeaning   b. unethical   c. mundane   d. uncontrollable

4. The author found that participants in edgework regard special "survival capacity" as:
   a. a gift from God   b. something everyone possesses
   c. an innate ability   d. a myth

5. When someone is killed or injured in a skydiving accident, it suggests to other participants in the sport that:
   a. more study and practice are needed
   b. the individual simply lacked "the right stuff"
   c. some risks in the sport are beyond anyone's ability to manage
   d. the individual's "number was up"

6. Although they practice very different forms of edgework, edgeworkers regard one another as:
   a. members of the same select group
   b. strangers   c. enemies   d. rivals

7. Experienced skydivers who have completed thousands of jumps report that:
   a. they are still fearful before reaching jump altitude
   b. after the first 100 jumps, there is less fun
   c. jumping is easier when one has had a few drinks
   d. they are fearful and full of tension and anxiety from the time they take off until their feet touch the ground

8. Despite the out-of-the-ordinary character of edgework, participants often describe their edgework experiences as:
   a. much more real than their day-to-day existence
   b. routine, and sometimes even boring
   c. just another job that anyone could perform
   d. something that requires little skill, concentration, or focused energy

9. What edgeworkers seem to value most is:
   a. "survival skill"   b. integrity   c. analytical reasoning
   d. cooperation

10. An edgeworker who is killed or injured by hazards that could have been avoided through planning and attention to standard precautions is:
    a. considered a hero   b. not much admired
    c. held up as a role model   d. a and c

II. True-False

129

F 1. Living in our society has grown increasingly dangerous.

T 2. According to Lyng, there is a public agenda in American society to reduce the risk of injury and death and a private agenda to increase such risks.

T 3. The concept of edgework can be extended to include hallucinogenic drug users and alcohol users who engage in binge drinking.

F 4. Lyng found that most people who are involved in edgework feel a deep sense of remorse and embarrassment about their activities.

T 5. Individuals who are accomplished in one type of edgework often try their hand at other types as well.

T 6. People who are negotiating the edge report that time passes either much faster or slower than usual.

F 7. A common side activity of edgeworkers is gambling.

T 8. The greatest satisfaction or feeling of competence for edgeworkers results from being able to control the seemingly uncontrollable.

III. Essay

1. Why are most edgeworkers not interested in gambling?
2. What motivates edgeworkers to seek out their experiences?
3. Explain the sense or illusion of control that develops among edgeworkers.
4. Compared with older adults, why are young adults better candidates for edgework?
5. Why are males more likely to become involved in edgework than females?

Article 38: Haas and Shaffir, "The Cloak of Competence"

I. Multiple-Choice

1. When someone is assumed to be competent and must act or make decisions affecting the well-being of others:
   a. managing impressions and role playing become significant, especially if there is a potentially critical audience
   b. managing impressions and role playing are relatively unimportant because credentials clarify the issue of competence
   c. competence is judged almost excusively on the basis of past performance
   d. competence is automatically assumed, and impression management has little influence on the assessment of competence
   e. there is such a severe testing process, both formal and informal, that none who are incompetent enter the role

2. Learning the language of medicine:
   a. comes fairly easily to medical students
   b. is not necessary because medical dictionaries are provided by the medical school
   c. is expensive, since special tutors must be hired
   d. is an essential part of the socialization into competence
   e. plays little role in the program at McMaster University, because this is an innovative teaching experiment

3. As medical students move through their program and develop a

professional self-image, they become:
a. more vocal in their questioning and criticisms of the medical profession
b. less vocal in their questioning and criticisms of the medical profession
c. less dependent upon the use of medical jargon
d. increasingly likely to develop warm, personal ties with patients, diminishing their tendency to objectify patients
e. less task-oriented and more idealistic

4. Medical students come to accept the view that it is necessary to depersonalize and objectify patients in order to:
a. keep them "in their place"
b. allow more leisure time for physicians
c. be able to charge the full amount
d. increase the physician's empathy with patients' symptoms
e. learn clinical symptoms and pathology

5. After a period of time in medical school, most students come to view emotional involvement with patients as:
a. a hinderance   b. necessary, but difficult
c. the "art" part of medical science
d. relatively easy for most students to attain
e. easier for female students to attain

6. As they are introduced gradually to the content and "core" of medicine, students begin to realize that:
a. they are incompetent
b. their undergraduate training was insufficient
c. there is too much to know and too little time in which to learn it
d. there is more to life than health
e. their professors do not know as much as they are supposed to

7. A strategy that students use to impress others that their competence is growing is to:
a. talk about how many medical books they have read
b. date only nurses
c. compare themselves to students who have failed
d. let others know how many autopsies they have assisted
e. ask questions for which they already know the answers

8. Adopting a cloak of competence is justified by students as helpful to patients because:
a. the patients then feel they are getting their money's worth
b. patients would be frightened if they thought their doctors did not know everything
c. if patients think the doctor is healing them, they might improve because of the placebo effect
d. many patients also read medical journals
e. none of the above

9. Objectifying patients and closing off feelings is viewed by advanced medical students as professionally:
a. appropriate, and helpful to patients
b. appropriate, but harmful to patients

c. inappropriate, but helpful to patients
d. inappropriate, and harmful to patients
e. deceptive to the doctors with whom they study

10. Students come to realize that an important part of becoming a physician is to:
    a. deceive the physicians with whom they study
    b. learn a role that projects an image of confidence
    c. stress the psychosocial aspects of medicine
    d. place the greatest emphasis on the psychosocial aspects of medicine
    e. keep themselves in mental, physical, and emotional shape

11. Impression management is basic and fundamental in those occupations and professions which:
    a. profess competence in matters seriously affecting others
    b. have vast reservoirs of information
    c. require state certification   d. are changing the most
    e. show the highest incidents of malpractice

12. To reduce the possibility of embarrassment and humiliation over their lack of medical knowledge, students:
    a. manipulate an impression of themselves as enthusiastic, interested, and eager to learn
    b. make certain others see them studying their medical textbooks
    c. avoid medical topics whenever they can
    d. sometimes pretend they have laryngitis and cannot answer questions
    e. are quick to point out that one of their parents (almost always the father) is a physician (which is often not the truth)

13. The data for this article were gathered by:
    a. the authors becoming students in a medical school
    b. the authors joining the faculty of a medical school
    c. participant observation and interviews
    d. a random survey of medical students in Canada
    e. a mailed questionnaire

II. True-False

T 1. Symbols such as lab jackets and name tags serve the dual functions of separating medical students from the lay world and, at the same time, uniting the bearers with one another.
F 2. As medical students devote more and more time and energy to their studies, they begin to seek out old friends and frantically pursue previous interests in order to escape total immersion in the world of medicine.
T 3. Linguistic symbols provide a means by which practicing physicians shape and control the definition of a situation.
T 4. Although they struggle against it, most medical students learn to accept the objectification of patients as a necessity.
F 5. Most medical students believe that they have time for both learning medicine and caring about patients.
F 6. Most medical students believe that emotional involvement with patients is an asset to their professional development.
T 7. Most medical students believe that "feeling" for their patients

(becoming emotionally involved with them) will hinder their becoming professionally competent.
T 8. Students justify their objectification of patients by emphasizing how much pathology they are learning and how much pressure they are under to master vast amounts of material in a limited time.
F 9. Because medical students recognize their low status in the hospital hierarchy, they tend to act incompetently, as they think this is how they are viewed by others. This is a type of self-fulfilling prophecy in professional development.
F 10. Although projecting a facade of competence is important to medical students, technical knowledge takes precedence.
T 11. Students come to the conclusion that to be a good student physician means either to be or appear to be competent.
F 12. According to Everett C. Hughes, it is a good rule to assume that a feature of work behavior found in one occupation is not likely to be found in others.
T 13. Medical students display their learning of medical jargon in order to create an imagery of authority and competence.
F 14. In order to help increase their efficiency in learning the vast body of medical knowledge that they must master, medical students drop their professional, scientific posturing.
F 15. The medical school studied by Haas and Shaffir stresses lectures, formal tests, and formal grades in the attempt to train good physicians.

III. Essay

1. Review the process by which medical students become detached from patients.
2. Discuss how (a) medical students acquire a cloak of competence, (b) this cloak is functional for physicians, (c) it can lead to unrealistic expectations on the part of both physicians and patients, and (d) it might affect medical care adversely.
3. Explain what the cloak of competence is and why you think this cloak is desirable or undesirable.

Article 39: Hunt, "Police Accounts of Normal Force"

I. Multiple-Choice

1. Police most often excuse morally problematic force by:
   a. "going on a rip" (getting "rip-roaring" drunk)
   b. going to confession   c. doing volunteer public service
   d. referring to emotional or physiological states
   e. pointing to the common wrongs and hypocrisies of the public

2. In this article, Hunt focuses on how force is seen by:
   a. the police themselves   b. reporters   c. prisoners
   d. the victims of violence   e. the clergy

3. The police perceive most acts of violence by the police that go beyond the law as:
   a. wrong   b. illegitimate   c. immoral   d. stupid
   e. normal

4. The police perceive brutality as:
   a. wrong   <u>b</u>. illegitimate   c. immoral   d. stupid
   e. normal

5. The data for this article were gathered by:
   a. newspaper accounts going back five years
   <u>b</u>. participant observation for 18 months
   c. interviews with prisoners   d. police informers
   e. interviews with the chiefs of police from ten major cities

6. In the police academy, police officers learn that they are
   permitted to use deadly force on or fire their revolvers at a
   suspect if and only if:
   a. the suspect resists arrest   b. restraint is clearly needed
   <u>c</u>. the officer is threatened with great bodily harm
   d. they receive permission from the suspect's mother
   e. they receive permission from higher authority in the police
      chain of command

7. The police in this report view the weapons issued by their
   department as unsatisfactory. This is indicated by:
   <u>a</u>. rookies replacing these weapons with more powerful ones
   b. the number of officers who signed a petition protesting the
      wooden baton and convoy jack
   c. the officers who, to make the point, brandished a toy weapon
      when the mayor was being interviewed by reporters
   d. part of their union negotiations being the demand for more
      powerful weapons and placed on par with the demand for higher
      wages
   e. the public demonstration after an officer was seriously injured
      when a department-issued revolver exploded in her hand

8. The contrast between the police subculture and the formal culture
   of the police academy is illustrated by this statement commonly
   expressed by the police:
   a. "once out of the academy, life is different"
   b. "never trust a rookie"
   <u>c</u>. "it's not done on the street the way it's taught at the
      academy"
   d. "never wear britches, they bring only stitches"
   e. "one for the money, and two for the gun, but ours is the only
      way it's done"

9. A brutality suit or a civilian complaint against an officer will
   have this effect on the officer's prestige among his or her peers:
   a. lower it   <u>b</u>. raise it   c. have no influence on it
   d. raise it only if the person bringing the suit is a minority
   e. lower it only if the person bringing the suit was injured

10. Officers who do not use force even when their own life is in
    jeopardy, but instead talk an armed suspect into surrendering,
    are:
    a. highly respected because they looked down the barrel of a gun
       and "didn't blink"
    b. often given commendations   c. sought after as partners
    d. a and c   <u>e</u>. the subject of degrading gossip

134

11. Police officers most often excuse their use of morally problematic force by referring to:
    a. the hostility of suspects   b. their own low salaries
    c. the bestiality of suspects   d. frustrations from the courts
    e. emotional or physiological states precipitated by their work

12. Police officers are more likely to excuse their use of force:
    a. when their personal identity is threatened
    b. when there is temporary loss of emotional control
    c. if the suspect has "gotten off easy" on some other occasion
    d. if the suspect is a minority
    e. if the police officer is new to the job

13. From the perspective of the police, almost anyone who verbally challenges the authority of a police officer is:
    a. an appropriate candidate for the use of force
    b. suspected of having committed crimes
    c. probably an undercover cop
    d. to be pitied   e. probably an educational failure

14. If a suspect attempts to sexualize an encounter with a female officer, it is likely to result in:
    a. the female officer seeking assistance from a male officer
    b. the female officer humoring the suspect
    c. the female officer using force to rectify insults and to establish control
    d. a male officer stepping in and using force on the spot
    e. a and d

15. Who is the most likely to have police force used against them?
    a. a man who has sexually molested a child
    b. high level mafioso   c. professional burglars   d. a "psycho"
    e. a man who has robbed and beaten a prostitute

16. What happened to the 17-year-old who raped a nun? The police:
    a. put his penis in an electrical outlet   b. shot him
    c. turned him over to the priests   d. castrated him
    e. recommended that he receive psychiatric treatment

II. True-False

F 1. The use of force is not at the core of the public mandate for the American police.
T 2. Although not always legitimate or admired, "cops" depict normal force as coercive acts that are a necessary or natural response of normal police to partricular situational exigencies.
F 3. When it comes to brutality, the police and the public are in general agreement regarding where to draw the line.
F 4. When it comes to the use of force, most street "cops" try to follow the standards set in the police academy.
F 5. When rookies become aggressive, veteran officers usually react with disdain and disapproval.
T 6. Peer approval helps to neutralize the guilt and overcome the confusion that rookies often experience when they begin to use force to assert their authority.

T 7. In order to become recognized as "real street cops," female
       rookies are encouraged by veteran officers to act more
       aggressively and to display more machismo than male rookies.
F 8. For a street cop, it is an error to use too much force rather
       than to use too little force, for he or she then risks
       developing a reputation as a "bad cop."
T 9. Even supervisors encourage new officers to adopt an attitude
       favorable to using less restraint when they use force.
F 10. Excuse is the term used for an account in which someone accepts
       full responsibility for an act but fails to acknowledge its
       appropriateness.
T 11. According to this article, the police always excuse force when
       it follows an experience of helplessness and confusion that has
       culminated in a temporary loss of emotional control.
F 12. In contrast to justifications, which are denials of responsi-
       bility for an act but recognize the act as blameworthy, excuses
       accept responsibility for the act but deny that the act is
       blameworthy.
T 13. The more morally reprehensible the act committed by a suspect,
       the more likely the police are to justify violence against the
       suspect.
T 14. The police seldom use force against "clean" criminals, such as
       high-level mafiosi, white-collar criminals, and professional
       burglars.

III. Essay

1. After defining normal force from the perspective of the police,
    explain how rookies are socialized into normal force.
2. Briefly explain the difference between excuses and justifications
    in the use of force.
3. Describe the standards or guidelines that the police use to draw
    the line between brutality and normal force.

Article 40: Mills, "The Structure of Power in American Society"

I. Multiple-Choice

1. Mills concludes that most Americans can be classified politically
    as:
    a. radical   b. liberal   c. reactionary   d. inactionary
    e. uninformed and naive

2. The following best describes Mills's interpretation of modern
    history:
    a. people have little control over history; it is adrift
    b. people are free to make history
    c. people are free to make history, but some are much freer than
       others
    d. if the United States continues on its present course, power to
       control history will diffuse more and more
    e. history is changing more rapidly than it used to

3. Mills argues that power has become concentrated into these
    institutions:
    a. political, military, economic   b. political, military, social

c. political, economic, social
d. medical, educational, and military
e. economic, political, and medical

4. The following characterizes Mills's analysis of the American economy:
   a. a permanent war economy
   b. an economy of small business entrepreneurs
   c. a private corporation economy   d. a and c   e. b and c

5. The following is not a member of the "power elite":
   a. the political directorate   b. the high military
   c. the party politicians   d. the corporate executive
   e. all are members of the power elite

6. Unity among the "power elite" is aided by:
   a. psychological and social similarities of the people involved
   b. similar mechanics of institutional hierarchies
   c. a willful attempt to consolidate power   d. all of the above
   e. none of the above

7. According to Mills, the "countervailing powers" and the "veto groups" of political parties and associations (labor unions, etc.) occupy this level of power:
   a. top   b. middle   c. lower   d. all of these
   e. none of these

8. In Mills's interpretation, the big decisions of international and national life such as war and peace, slums and poverty, are made by:
   a. the political parties   b. debates in Congress
   c. an oligarchy of powerful men   d. the American electorate
   e. the President

9. Mills is convinced that Congress exists at this level of power:
   a. lower   b. top   c. middle
   d. this varies with the party in power
   e. he does not deal with Congress in his analysis

10. With the increasing size of mass political organizations and associations, which of the following is most true about the subsequent influence of individuals within those associations?
    a. the influence of the individual is on the increase
    b. the influence of the individual is on the decrease
    c. individuals can accomplish little collectively
    d. the collective good that is achieved primarily ensures individual benefit
    e. they are banding together to achieve greater power

11. The major representatives of the old independent middle class, which maintained "political balance" in past America, were:
    a. farmers and small businessmen   b. factory workers
    c. corporate leaders   d. the unskilled workers
    e. ranchers and farmers

12. To Mills "the public" has become:

a. rather enlightened partisan voters
b. vague, noninvolved masses of people
c. remnants of the old middle class whose interests are explicitly
   defined and organized
d. a broad electorate   e. sedentary because of television

13. According to Mills, public opinion is increasingly controlled by:
    a. traditional values
    b. enlightened awareness and discussion of the issues that control
       human destiny
    c. politicians and party ideas   d. the mass media   e. teachers

14. Mills sees the development of democracy in America in terms of:
    a. a decreasing involvement and interest in political power by the
       public
    b. an increasing involvement and interest in power by the public
    c. the eventual natural decline of the "power elite"
    d. a movement toward more participatory democracy
    e. an outgrowth of European movements

15. Mills predicts that this level of American society will become
    increasingly unified:
    a. the top   b. the middle   c. the bottom
    d. the working class
    e. Mills predicts greater diversity within all levels of American
       society because of the increasing tensions that we are
       experiencing

II. True-False

T 1. According to Mills, the basic problem of power is the problem
       of who makes the decisions about the arrangements under which
       people live.
T 2. Mills characterizes Western societies today as being largely
       devoid of ideological convictions and plagued by a prevalence
       of mass indifference.
F 3. Compared with other periods of history, power is now becoming
       more diffuse.
T 4. World War II helped firm the connections between business and
       government.
T 5. Mills argues that the United States does not have suitable
       agencies and traditions for the democratic handling of
       international affairs.
T 6. Mills says that virtually all political and military actions
       are now judged in terms of military definitions of reality.
F 7. Mills argues that politics is the areana in which free and
       independent organizations connect the lower and middle levels
       of society with the top levels of decision making.
T 8. Mills sees the typical labor leader of today as merely an
       adaptive creature of the main business life of corporate
       America.
F 9. To Mills, the phrase "governmentalization of the lobby" refers
       to the failure of interest groups to adequately represent their
       unique concerns.
T 10. Mills argues that public influence and opinion are largely
       guided by the mass communication media.

138

F 11. Mills would say that in spite of the emergence of a "power
       elite," the issues that shape human fate are still raised and
       decided by the public at large.
F 12. Mills is confident that the public will rise and halt the
       growing coalescence of power by the elite he describes.

III. Essay

1. List and describe recent historical events that support the
    position that Congress does not act at the highest power level but
    seems caught in "inaction." List and describe recent historical
    events that support the thesis that Congress "acts" in a deter-
    minative fashion, contrary to Mills. Evaluate the argument.
2. If you were assigned the project of validating or invalidating
    Mills's hypothesis of the existence of a "power elite," what kinds
    of data or information would you seek? Where might you find such
    data?

Introduction to Part IX: "Social Change"

I. Multiple-Choice

1. Which of the following may be the maxim under which living
    creatures exist?
    a. "struggle and create"   b. "failure breeds success"
    c. "adapt or die"
    d. "Do unto others as you would have them do unto you"
    e. "peace and love"

2. The difference between social change in the ancient world and
    social change today is:
    a. change primarily affected the rich of the ancient world, but
       now it affects everyone
    b. change primarily affected the poor of the ancient world, but
       now it affects everyone
    c. there was more social change in the ancient world than in our
       world
    d. change is faster now
    e. change was more erractic in the ancient world

3. Concerning parents and children today:
    a. social change tends to separate them into different worlds of
       reality
    b. social change is so rapid that today children look less like
       their parents than was the case only a couple of generations
       ago
    c. with our current social change, children are playing less than
       they used to, and the parents are acquiescing to this change
    d. with our current social change, parents are not as good at
       parenting as they used to be
    e. many children have become so disobedient, and many parents so
       calloused, that the world is going to hell in a handbasket

4. In general, confronted with challenge, humans:

a. become cautious
b. females faint, while men show their shock differently
<u>c</u>. adapt   d. retreat   e. slow down

II. True-False

T 1. Barring catastrophe, social change in ancient times was slow
       and orderly.
T 2. Social change tends to separate generations into different
       worlds of reality.
T 3. Only organisms that adapt to changing circumstance survive, and
       humans are no exception.
F 4. Contemporary change is affecting primarily the social institu-
       tions of society and the outward behaviors of people. Social
       change seldom affects people's ideas and beliefs, the
       fundamental concepts that make up their basic orientation to
       the world.
F 5. Humans are failing to change their social institutions to match
       changed circumstances.
F 6. Social change is primarily a contemporary phenomenon; social
       change was not a part of ancient civilization.

Article 41: Murray, "The Abolition of <u>El</u> <u>Cortito</u>"

I. Multiple-Choice

1. The term <u>El</u> <u>Cortito</u> refers to:
    <u>a</u>. a short-handled hoe
    b. a haircut associated with radical Hispanic reformers
    c. the river which forms the border between California and Mexico
    d. a 16th-century conquistador whose ruthlessness and name are
       associated with starving masses

2. The abolition of <u>El</u> <u>Cortito</u> is an example of:
    <u>a</u>. the mobilization of state institutions to bring about social
       change
    b. the use of terrorist tactics to bring about social change
    c. social change resulting from interracial marriages
    d. the erosion of traditional values and morals

3. <u>El</u> <u>Cortito</u> is of _____ origin:
    a. Mexican   <u>b</u>. Japanese   c. Appalachian   d. Canadian

4. In California during the second decade of the 20th century,
    Japanese agricultural workers replaced these agricultural workers:
    a. Irish   <u>b</u>. Mexican   c. Chinese   d. Blacks

5. The growers were not concerned about the effects of <u>El</u> <u>Cortito</u> on
    the workers' health because they:
    a. did not know about it--this was not medically demonstrated until
       1987
    b. had a steady supply of cheap labor that could be relied upon to
       replace injured workers
    c. thought that it increased productivity
    <u>d</u>. b and c

6. The kind of labor performed by workers using El Cortito is called:
    a. stooge labor   b. scab labor   c. short labor
    d. stoop labor

7. Farm workers in California gained support from this (these) group(s):
    a. the AFL-CIO   b. urban liberals   c. students
    d. all of the above

8. In 1970, a nationwide boycott against this product signaled a significant shift in relations between agribusiness and farm laborers:
    a. sugar beets   b. lettuce   c. grapes   d. olives

9. One result of the ban on El Cortito is that:
    a. growers now have more respect for workers
    b. with fewer injuries, union organizers can build a base for support among workers over entire seasons
    c. it caused the price of farm produce such as lettuce to double
    d. problems with crop infestation by insects increased

10. Lessons from El Cortito are being applied to this issue:
    a. working during foul weather   b. ozone exposure
    c. exposure to hazardous pesticides
    d. repetitive motions of laborers in the salmon canning industry that result in joint and nerve damage

II. True-False

T 1. Japanese farm workers in California were tightly organized with in-depth knowledge about intensive cultivation.
T 2. The large numbers of campesinos from Mexico who arrived in California came in search of work or to escape political persecution.
F 3. The campesinos insisted on using El Cortito in order to decrease productivity.
T 4. Growers prefer high turnover among their workers.
F 5. Dustbowl migrants of the Depression waged the first successful battles in the war to organize farm workers in California.
T 6. The Office of Economic Opportunity was created under President Johnson to meet and channel the demands of social unrest.
T 7. The argument that workers who are injured through the use of El Cortito would become burdens to the taxpayer was used successfully in linking the case with a broader constituency.
T 8. The use of El Cortito was ultimately determined to be "a violation of safety."

III. Essay

1. What were the arguments of the growers and those who worked with El Cortito? Show how their positions depended on their economic circumstances.
2. Explain how El Cortito was banned. Be sure to include the forces that became aligned with one another.
3. From this material, what can you say about social change? Be sure to discuss resistance to social change and the factors that help

overcome this resistance.

Article 42: Ouchi, "Decision-Making in Japanese Organizations"

I. Multiple-Choice

1. When an important decision needs to be made in a Japanese organi-
    zation:
    a. everyone who will feel its impact is involved in making the
       decision
    b. the CEO makes the decision
    c. the CEO and the vice president make the decision
    d. secrecy is maintained until the decision has been reached by
       upper-level management; then a directive is sent downward

2. When a major decision needs to be made in a Japanese business, a
    written proposal lays out the "best" alternative for considera-
    tion. This proposal is written by:
    a. the person with the most seniority
    b. the youngest and newest member of the department involved
    c. the CEO of the business
    d. every member of the department involved

3. In a Japanese organization, formal proposals are circulated from
    the:
    a. CEO downward
    b. board of directors to the CEO and then downward
    c. bottom to the top
    d. middle and then upward and downward simultaneously

4. Western decision-making teams are deliberately kept small because:
    a. people in the West have diverse underlying values and beliefs
    b. of elitist views that only those at the top have significant
       insight
    c. American business managers don't want to emulate the Japanese
    d. it is felt fewer women will become involved if participation is
       limited

5. The most notable economic challenge to the United States comes
    from:
    a. Mexico   b. Great Britain   c. Russia   d. Japan

6. The evidence strongly suggests that a consensus approach to
    decision-making leads to:
    a. hard feelings and misunderstandings among employees
    b. more creative decisions   c. chaos and lost time
    d. political maneuvers and behind-the-scenes manipulation on the
       part of managers

7. When a decision is made through the consensual approach:
    a. there is more understanding and support for it
    b. it takes less time
    c. employees are more likely to be disgruntled about changes
    d. employees tend to be less informed

8. In Japanese organizations, responsibility is:

142

a. intentionally ambiguous
b. strictly divided so that crystal-clear boundaries separate areas of authority
c. not shared by team members, but instead designated to members of the department who have the most seniority
d. shirked whenever possible

9. In a Japanese organization, if one team member is unable to work:
a. he or she is fired
b. other team members are resentful and assign the most difficult tasks to the individual when he or she returns
c. there is a bottleneck in the operation which results in drastically reduced productivity
d. other members take up his or her share of the work load

10. In Japanese organizations, short-run labor needs can be filled without having to hire and fire people because:
a. all departments are padded with more labor than they actually need
b. they expect productivity to rise and fall, based upon short-term market forces
c. a volunteer labor force of retired employees steps in to assist the organization
d. of the practice of job rotation within the organization

II. True-False

T 1. Sociologists use the term "social system" to refer to the intercommunications that make people and organizations part of the same network.
F 2. "Participative decision-making" is one of the essential aspects of the German decision-making process.
F 3. The consensus approach to decision-making yields confusion, making it difficult to develop creative decisions.
F 4. Decision-making by consensus takes less time than individual decision-making.
T 5. Within Japanese organizations what is important is not the decision itself but rather how committed and informed people are.
T 6. A key feature of decision-making in Japan is the intentional ambiguity of who is responsible for what decisions.
F 7. In Japan, there are crystal-clear boundaries of where one person's authority over a particular turf ends and where another person's begins.
F 8. One of the major complaints that Americans have about doing business with the Japanese is that while the Japanese are quick to make decisions they are slow in implementing them.
T 9. The Japanese management system relies on trust developed through intimacy.

III. Essay

1. How do American businesspersons view the time it takes for decisions to be made within a Japanese organization?
2. What are the major differences between how decisions are made in Japanese organizations and in American organizations?

3. What element(s) of American culture make it difficult to implement participative decision-making?

Article 43:   Zuboff, "New Worlds of Computer-Mediated Work"

I. Multiple-Choice

1. In the 1860s, a proposal for _____ was met with extreme resistance by textile workers.
   a. reduced wages   b. being chained to the textile machines
   c. no work, no pay   d. collective work hours   e. child labor

2. Zuboff says that _____ has brought about fundamental changes in the way people think about work behavior.
   a. toxification   b. intoxification   c. intoxication
   d. patronization   e. industrialization

3. _____, workers have developed elaborate grievance procedures and work rules limiting an employer's right to control a worker's body:
   a. Through collective bargaining   b. In communist countries
   c. While employers created new benefits for older workers
   d. While new employees rejected new benefits for older workers
   e. While older workers rejected new benefits

4. During periods of technological transition, workers are likely to:
   a. articulate about the quality of the change they are facing
   b. feel that the technology conflicts with their expectations of the workplace
   c. resist the new technology   d. all of the above
   e. none of the above

5. Zuboff based her article on:
   a. interviews with about 200 employees, supervisors, profes-sionals, and managers
   b. questionnaires distributed to government employees
   c. the experiences of Harvard University in installing its first centrally automated computerized system
   d. a survey of articles in The Reader's Guide to Popular Literature
   e. none of the above

6. The term "computer mediated" means:
   a. measured more accurately in metrics through the use of a computer
   b. a person accomplishes a task through the medium of a computer-ized information system
   c. that in order to contact an individual a person first must get authorization from a computer which serves as a "middle man"
   d. a computer registers the kilowatts and issues accounts based on megacycles of one hundred
   e. meditation that is initiated or encouraged through a computer

7. Zuboff points out that making tasks computer-mediated often:
   a. leads to frustration for workers because the workers lose direct experience with the tasks they perform

b. increases satisfaction of workers because computers make fewer errors than humans, and workers can often use the line, "Sorry, the computer is down," as an excuse when they get behind in their work
c. increases direct experiences with tasks, especially in highly complex work
d. sells a lot of computers
e. makes the skills of college graduates obsolate in 18 months

8. The comptroller of a bank said that introducing information systems to a bank causes people to:
   a. become more technical and sophisticated as they develop a superior understanding of the banking business
   b. throw monkey wrenches into the new system in order to go back to the old ways
   c. become more technical and sophisticated, but to develop an inferior understanding of the banking business
   d. move rapidly up the ladder of banking success
   e. none of the above

9. When information technology permits a clerical worker to complete an entire operation at his or her own work station, rather than completing part of the procedure and then passing the work on to someone else, the result is:
   a. a fragmentation of the social network
   b. increased feelings of solidarity among co-workers because fewer workers are giving work to one another
   c. a questioning of where authority is really coming from since workers are giving each other fewer orders and instructions
   d. more interaction among workers due to increased leisure
   e. increased profits to the employer, increased dividends to the owners, and more bonuses to the workers

10. Computer conferencing:
    a. restricts co-worker contact   b. usually fails
    c. makes it easier to initiate dialogues and form coalitions with workers in other parts of the corporation
    d. works best among lower-level staff   e. lowers worker morale

11. With respect to the control of workers by supervisors, information technology:
    a. restricts the monitoring of worker performance
    b. makes it virtually impossible to monitor worker performance
    c. greatly enhances the ability of supervisors to monitor workers --even without their knowledge
    d. gives workers more control   e. a and d

12. When computer systems are used to monitor work performance, workers:
    a. prefer this system to human supervisors because they feel the computer system is unbiased and objective
    b. relax and feel more in control of their work
    c. decrease their productivity, but no one yet knows why
    d. find that promotions come easier
    e. prefer human supervisors so they can negotiate and argue

13. When information technology is introduced into a work setting, it usually affects feelings of:
   a. romance   b. intimacy   c. power
   d. the more dishonest workers   e. masculinity and femininity

14. Zuboff reports that in the view of many managers and professionals, information systems:
   a. limit their freedom   b. augment their power
   c. limit their opportunity for creative decisions
   d. all of the above   e. none of the above

15. When a computer system was installed in the Volvo plant in Kalmar, Sweden, to monitor assembly operations by flashing a red light to signal a problem in quality control, the workers:
   a. insisted that the task be returned to a foreman
   b. received large bonuses as the quality of their work improved
   c. began to slack off in their work as the computer let much sloppier work go through than had the supervisor
   d. found that the assembly line was also speeded up
   e. had a difficult time finding slack periods for coffee breaks

II. True-False

T 1. New forms of technology inevitably change the ways in which people are mobilized to work as well as the kinds of skills and behavior that are critical for productivity.
F 2. Even if people feel that the demands that a new technology makes on them conflict with their expectations about the workplace, they are not likely to resist during the initial stage of adaptation.
F 3. During a period of technological transition, people are not likely to be aware of or to articulate about the quality of change they are facing.
T 4. Even though employees may accommodate the demands of a new technology, unresolved original sources of resistance may influence the management-labor relationship for years.
F 5. The increased use of information technology does not greatly affect the technological infrastructure of the workplace.
T 6. Word processing and electronic mail are examples of information technology.
F 7. White-collar workers are almost the only ones who interact with computers in the workplace.
F 8. Decision-making is one function that computers cannot take over.
F 9. Auditing is one example of a highly individualized technical skill that cannot be altered through the use of information technology.
T 10. Once information technology reorganizes a set of jobs, new patterns of communication and interaction are likely to alter the social structure of an organization.
T 11. Information technology alters relations between managers by making managers reluctant to make decisions on the basis of information that they and their superiors receive simultaneously.
F 12. Zuboff points out that technology is neutral.

146

1. Explain how information technology makes some workers feel a sense of isolation, and how in some instances information technology causes a breakdown in the worker community.
2. Explain how information technology influences the rate of productivity in the workplace.
3. Discuss how information technology makes tangible work abstract.
4. Discuss the implications of information technology for human relationships in the workplace.
5. Discuss why managers are reluctant to make decisions on the basis of information that they and their superiors receive simultaneously.

Article 44: Rodriguez, "Searching for Roots in a Changing World"

I. Multiple-Choice

1. According to the introduction to this article, the attempt to "better oneself," to climb another rung on the social ladder, is one of the basic reasons for:
   a. our high rate of suicide   b. our high rate of mental illness
   c. the impersonality and "coldness" of our society
   d. our high rate of violent crimes   e. American restlessness

2. Rodriguez states that his parents had to give this up although it was central to the intimacy that his family felt in an otherwise alien world:
   a. extended relationships   b. Mexican culinary customs
   c. speaking Spanish   d. their children, including himself
   e. the security of their pension

3. Rodriguez states that this was the most dramatic and obvious indication that he would become very much like a "gringo":
   a. speaking English instead of Spanish
   b. following Anglo food customs   c. marrying an Anglo girl
   d. wearing a suit and tie
   e. refusing to take high school courses in auto mechanics

4. Rodriguez says that nearly every other minority student he had known in graduate school dropped out because of:
   a. their graduation from barrio high schools
   b. lack of intelligence   c. lack of fluency in English
   d. financial pressures   e. cultural reasons

5. When Rodriguez began to yearn for the very Chicano culture that he had abandoned as useless, he felt:
   a. a surge of renewed energy   b. elated
   c. full of future shock   d. depressed   e. fearful

6. Rodriguez feels that he has experienced:
   a. future shock   b. rational order   c. culture loss
   d. the best medical program available in American universities
   e. a balanced education

7. At the end of this article, as Rodriguez is being interviewed for

a job teaching English at a university, he feels a desire for:
a. a position with more money
b. a job that allows him to teach medieval romantic literature
c. a job at a more prestigious university
d. teaching the modern Chicano novel   e. the past

8. Rodriguez's basic feeling towards his Chicano past is:
a. hostility and resentment   b. superiority of the present
c. pity for those who couldn't climb the ladder of success
d. a longing for it, to be a part of it
e. a desire to separate himself even further from it

II. True-False

T 1. Americans are among the most geographically mobile of all people.
F 2. On the average, perhaps forty percent of our population changes residence each year.
T 3. Rodriguez states that through his education, he has lost at least as much as he has gained.
F 4. Rodriguez states that he was forced to give up his Chicano past.
T 5. Rodriguez states that education led him to "repudiate his race."
F 6. Rodriguez states that, with so many fellow Chicanos in the university, he had a chance to develop an alternative consciousness.
T 7. Rodriguez found that there was no possibility of going back to what he had been before he became an academic.
T 8. Rodriguez states that he has lost the ability to bring his past into his present.
F 9. One could fairly conclude from this article that Rodriguez is content with the effects of his education.
F 10. During the educational process Rodriguez began to feel cut off from his Chicano roots. When he discovered Chicano literature, however, he was able to merge his roots with his educational goals.
F 11. Rodriguez considers himself a Chicano intellectual.

III. Essay

1. Almost inevitably, social mobility brings pain. In this article, Rodriguez gives us the picture from the point of view of a child who has left his parents behind as he experienced upward mobility. Why does social mobility often entail such personal pain?
2. Explain how it would be possible for Rodriguez to complete his Ph.D., teach in a college or university, and still maintain a Chicano identity.

NOTES

NOTES

NOTES

NOTES